I0416807

TABLE OF CONTENTS

INTRODUCTION

This nation is peaceful, but fierce when stirred to anger. The conflict was begun on the timing and terms of others. It will end in a way, and at an hour, of our choosing.[1]

> President Bush
> The National Cathedral, Washington, D.C.
> September 14, 2001

Nature of the problem

The Al Qaeda Network is a global insurgency; however, the United States and much of the western world continues to identify it as a "global terrorist organization." This improper label misleads leaders in the development of effective strategic and operational level plans. As a result, the national strategy and operational approach are not properly focused. The nation must recognize Al Qaeda as a global insurgency and adjust both the national strategy and the accompanying operational approach accordingly. The country has failed to adhere to one of Clausewitz's first maxims; it has not properly . . . defined the war in which it is involved.

The Al Qaeda Network has declared war against the western world and specifically against the U.S. Its short term goals include the establishment of an Islamic Caliphate through violent action and the removal of all western presence in Islamic lands, to include "apostate" governments which they feel have been corrupted by their links with the western world. Its long term goals include the violent expansion of that caliphate throughout the world and the conversion of all peoples to Islam. To achieve its goals, it has established a global insurgency that often uses terrorist tactics. Its use of these tactics has led the U.S. and much of the international community to mischaracterize them as a "terrorist organization." This definition only speaks to a portion of the nature of the organization and using it limits true understanding of

---

[1] President George Bush, "Speech at the National Cathedral" (Speech, Washington, D.C., 14 September 2001).

the real problem. The U.S. approach to defeating Al Qaeda suffers in effectiveness due to this lack of understanding of it as a global insurgent network.

Charlie Szrom and Chris Harnisch, in *A New Approach to the War on Terror*, describe the U.S. policy and approach towards Al Qaeda as a "strategy of tactics," using a phrase that Andrew Krepinevich used when describing the U.S. approach towards Vietnam.[2] While several administrations have attempted to address Al Qaeda, none have developed a comprehensive approach based on an accurate classification of the organization. It is crucial to understand the Al Qaeda Network from the perspective of a global insurgency in order to develop an effective approach to defeat it.

The environment has changed significantly over the past year with respect to the Al Qaeda Network and the U.S. position relative to them. Usama bin Laden's death, and the recent deaths of other senior Al Qaeda leaders over the past few years, has changed the nature of the network. Al Qaeda will be more difficult to predict since they will be led by lesser known personalities, which may complicate the future. However, this new dynamic also represents a renewed opportunity to gain ground against its international operations and potentially gain traction in actually defeating it instead of merely conducting a long term disruption operation against it. Focused efforts across the full spectrum of national power can have a significant effect on the network in the next few years. To do this, the U.S. must redefine Al Qaeda, appropriately identify its weaknesses, and shift the main effort from a direct approach to a comprehensive, whole of government, indirect approach.

To accomplish the goal of defeating Al Qaeda and its associated movements, the U.S. must change its strategy towards, and execution of, the fight against it from a counterterrorism-

---

[2] Charlie Szrom and Chris Harnsich, *Al Qaeda's Operating Environment: A New Approach to the War on Terror* (American Enterprise Institute, March 2011), 4.

centric to a counterinsurgency-centric approach. Terrorism is a tactic, not a strategy. So who or what is the nation fighting? Why? And how should they be doing it? By ignoring the fact that the Al Qaeda Network is a global insurgency using terrorist tactics, the U.S. limits its ability to develop a holistic solution to defeat and destroy, rather than simply disrupt, the network. The nation must adopt a new approach centered on an indirect approach, a focus on the ideology, aggressive diplomacy, increased diplomatic and developmental capacity, and a clear comprehensive strategy to support all of it. This paper will define the nature of Al Qaeda, assess the drawbacks of the current strategy, and propose methods to improve the United States' approach to defeating them.

Today's Muslim world stretches from the Philippine Islands to Morocco, and from Southern Russia to Central Africa. Beyond that, there are now Muslims in many of the countries of the western world. There were 1.6B Muslims in 2010 and they accounted for 23% of the world's population.[3] They are projected to continue growing both in population and percentage at least through 2030.[4] Even if not for the current threat from the Al Qaeda Network, the Muslim world would warrant significant attention just based on their contributions to the global environment as well as the challenges they face. Many of the countries with Muslim majorities suffer from high unemployment, inadequate economic development, poor governance, and heavily imbalanced wealth distribution. All of these factors result in understandable anger and frustration on the part of the population. Exacerbating these frustrations and adding to the sense of humiliation is a Muslim history that includes the fall of the Ottoman Empire and the resulting decline of the Islamic position in the world. All of this has been exacerbated over the past

---

[3] Pew Research Center publications, *The Future of the Global Muslim Population: Projections for 2010-2030,* (Online at Pew Research Center website, January 27, 2011, accessed on February 12, 2012 from http://pewresearch.org/pubs/1872/muslim-population-projections-worldwide-fast-growth).
    [4] Ibid.

several decades by U.S. support to repressive authoritarian regimes that, from the U.S. perspective, represent stability and counterterrorism partnerships in Muslim countries. All of this adds up to an environment ripe for violent extremists to blend an already harsh reality with some untruths and some very loose interpretations of the Koran, into a narrative that fosters hatred towards the U.S.

The Need for a New Approach

The national strategy for defeating Al Qaeda, and the implementation of that strategy, must shift from the current approach to one founded on a more accurate characterization of the network with a greater focus on the integration of all of the instruments of national power. The new approach must deviate from the current direct, enemy-centric counterterrorism campaign, to a more indirect, population-centric, global counterinsurgency. The country must develop a policy of more aggressive diplomacy towards militant Islamists as well as the rest of the Muslim world. The capacity and resources of both the Department of State and the Unites States Agency for International Development must be increased. The main effort must focus on Al Qaeda's ideology, militant Islamism, rather than the operational aspects of the network. Finally, this must be a truly comprehensive whole of government approach that leverages the unique capabilities and specialties of each department or agency, rather than defaulting to one department (DoD) because it has greater capacity.

This paper will review the current national policy on counterterrorism and the state of Al Qaeda and its associated movements prior to Usama bin Laden's death. It will then look at the changes in Al Qaeda and assess the impacts those changes will have on its ability to achieve its objectives. This will be followed by an analysis of the effectiveness of the current fight against Al Qaeda, leading to the determination that the network is a global insurgency rather than a "terrorist organization." The current approach will then be evaluated against the tenets of counterinsurgency. This analysis will be followed by a series of recommendations at the strategic and operational levels and further divided into defense, diplomacy, and development categories.

This paper will remain at the unclassified level in order to broaden its distribution. This restriction limited the research materials available and also limited the discussion of ongoing activities. However, most of the classified activities fall into the realm of the military and the intelligence organizations which, as the paper will demonstrate, are important to the defeating Al Qaeda, but should not be the main effort.

This page intentionally left blank

CHAPTER 1: AL QAEDA (OLD AND NEW)

Know Your Enemy: The Al Qaeda Network Defined

Who is the enemy: Al Qaeda, Militant Islam, Violent Extremist Organizations, Terrorism, Islamism . . . Islam itself? There is little agreement on how to acknowledge and describe publically and completely who the "enemy" really is. The U.S. must first clearly understand who and what it is fighting, and why it is fighting them, in order to defeat this enemy. The events of 9/11 led the U.S. into the "War on Terrorism," which was eventually refined into a war on Al Qaeda. Around the world today there are a large number of Muslim groups, some of whom are beneficial actors in their communities supporting universal rights and freedoms, some definitely not. The U.S. perception depends on with whom they are allied at the time, with whom the U.S. is allied at the time, and who their common enemies might be. This chapter will take a brief look at what the Al Qaeda Network is, examine the evolution of the ideology behind it, and analyze the threat it represents to the security of the U.S. and its national interests. It will conclude by identifying the real threat facing the western world with respect to Al Qaeda in order to redefine the problem and begin developing a more comprehensive and appropriate approach.

The Al Qaeda network is a global association of militant Islamist extremists who are waging a coordinated series of simultaneous regional and country level insurgencies with the intent of establishing a global caliphate. They seek to impose their ideology on the world by seizing political power through a violent insurgency. One government paper describes them as "an enemy that holds a totalitarian ideology and seeks to impose that ideology through force across the globe."[1] Al Qaeda is, and must be recognized and treated as, a global insurgency fighting for control of the world's Muslim population and the elimination of western society.

---

[1] U.S. Department of Homeland Security, *Terminology to Define the Terrorists: Recommendations from American Muslims* (Washington, D.C.: Department of Homeland Security, January 2008), 1.

Al Qaeda Before May 2011

Al Qaeda has been given numerous labels since its inception, some self-appointed and some given to it from external elements. The most common label used is that "Al Qaeda is a revolutionary salafist mujahedin terrorist organization."[2] It purports to believe in a better world achieved through the rejection of temptation. It feeds off of the underlying emotions in the Muslim world that stem from perceptions of humiliation and degradation in comparison to developed western countries. It carefully and deliberately fuels these emotions with a narrative based on a misinterpretation of the history and interaction between the Muslim and non-Muslim worlds.[3]

Many scholars address the Al Qaeda Network, and the rest of the Muslim world, in the post-9/11 context. It is important to remember that Al Qaeda existed before 9/11; it formed in 1988 and began conducting attacks in earnest in the mid-1990s. Further, the pre-conditions within the Muslim community, which allowed Al Qaeda to gain support and flourish, existed well before 9/11. As the 9/11 commission's report mentions, "bin Laden and other Islamist terrorist leaders draw on a long tradition of extreme intolerance" within a minority stream of Islam, which is fed by grievances widely felt throughout the Muslim world.[4] The militant Islamist beliefs, as espoused by this minority stream, not only blend religion and politics, but do not distinguish between the two, and in fact advocate the use of violence to achieve their religious and political goals. The 9/11 Commission further broke down the threat by distinguishing between the global Al Qaeda Network and "a radical ideological movement in the Islamic world, inspired in part by Al Qaeda, which has spawned terrorist groups and violence

---

[2] Blake Ward, "Osama's Wake: The Second Generation of Al Qaeda," *Counterproliferation Papers, Future Warfare Series,* Future Warfare Series , no. 32 (August 2005): 1.
[3] Ibid., 5.
[4] National Commission on Terrorist Attacks upon the United States, *The 9/11 Commission Report: Final Report of the National Commission on Terrorist Attacks Upon on the United States* (New York: Norton, 2004), 362.

across the globe."[5] This distinction demonstrates one of the many reasons why simply eliminating all of the current members of Al Qaeda will not solve the problem. They are a symptom, and the United States and the rest of the western world must treat the cause. The U.S. must fight the ideological foundation from which Al Qaeda gains its credibility, support, funding, and replacements in order to truly destroy it.

In order to understand the Muslim frustrations that Al Qaeda has been so adroitly exploiting, it is important to understand the pre-conditions that led to them. These pre-conditions were founded in the 7th century when the Islamic Prophet Muhammad blended the political and religious arenas and the lack of clear direction or foundation within the religion that followed his death. Whether he intended to or not, by simultaneously serving as the political leader and the religious leader he created a pattern of political-religious governance, which has endured in various forms to the present. Muslims look to their history to demonstrate how this model served them well since the seventh century. This culminated with the Ottoman Empire, which stood shoulder to shoulder with the European powers of its time. The last century saw the fall of Ottoman Empire, although it began its decline somewhere around the end of the 17th century depending to which theory one subscribes. After being described as "the present terror of the world" by Richard Knolles in 1603, it reached a turning point when Grand Vizier Merzifonlu Kara Mustafa Pasha was defeated in Vienna in 1683, marking the end of Ottoman expansion into Europe. The Ottoman decline was completed in the early 20th century when it was divided by the victors after it allied itself with Germany during World War I. Usama bin Laden referred to this subjugation of Muslims to western powers in several writings and speeches.[6] The reference

---

[5] Ibid., 363.

[6] Usama bin Laden, "Declaration of jihad against the United States," (originally posted on the Al-Islah website on September 2, 1996, accessed on February 21, 2012 from http://www.pbs.org/newshour/terrorism/international/fatwa_1996.html) and Usama bin Laden, "Jihad Against Jews

was easily understood by Muslims and played well on old emotional scars. Conversely, most western leaders had a hard time understanding why events of almost a century ago still evoked such a deep emotional reaction. This further speaks to the U.S. cultural misunderstanding in its application of the instruments of national power.

More recent events of the past few decades have been incorporated into Al Qaeda's narrative as emotional ammunition. Michael Scheuer makes this case in several books saying that, "the focused and lethal threat posed to U.S. national security arises not from Muslims being offended by what America is, but rather from their plausible perception that the things they most love and value—God, Islam, their brethren, and Muslim lands—are being attacked by America."[7] If this is in fact the perception of the Muslim world, then this is what the U.S. must fight, not the tactical fight in which it wants to engage. This is where attempts to recite U.S. positive contributions to Muslim countries and communities falls short. By understanding their mindset, the U.S. can begin to target policies appropriately to change their perceptions in order to develop positive and productive relationships with moderate Muslims so that they will take it upon themselves to seek out the extremists elements and eliminate the support that those elements need to survive. Scheuer goes on to draw a distinction from the more common belief, as espoused by Samuel Huntington in *Clash of Civilizations*, that the Al Qaeda's confrontation with the United States is founded purely in religious and cultural differences. This leads one to the conclusion, advocated by Scheuer, that they "hate us for what we do," not "who we are."[8] This statement runs counter to many in the U.S. who assume that the country is involved in a clash of civilizations in which there is no solution other than to force Muslims to accept

---

and Crusaders," (originally published by the al Quds al Arabi newspaper on February 23, 1998, accessed on February 21, 2012 from http://www.pbs.org/newshour/terrorism/international/fatwa_1998.html).
    [7] Michael Scheuer, *Imperial Hubris: Why the West is Losing the War on Terror* (Washington, DC: Potomac Books Inc, 2004), 9.
    [8] Ibid., 8.

coexistence with western culture. When viewed through the lens provided by Scheuer, that of the Muslim perspective, it becomes more clear where the frustrations began and why they continue to this day. While this understanding in no way confers legitimacy to their actions, it provides context for western understanding and provides a more clear start point for a new engagement strategy towards Muslims.

The actions in question include America's seemingly unquestioning support for Israel; relationships with regionally stabilizing regimes that repress their own populations such as Egypt (before the revolution), Kuwait, Algeria, Saudi Arabia and others; support for India against Muslim insurgents in Kashmir; and the American military presence in Saudi Arabia. These actions, coupled with a negative perception of Christianity and Western European powers generated by the Crusades of the 11th, 12th, and 13th centuries, have contributed to a Muslim perception of U.S. (which it sees as the leader of the primarily Judeo-Christian western world) bias in its current foreign policy. While not part of the original justification for their hatred, the wars in Afghanistan and Iraq have played well in their narrative of western aggression against Islam. Al Qaeda has been able to leverage the emotions and frustrations brought about by these actions, in the context of the historical interaction between the Muslim and non-Muslim worlds, to fuel the Muslim anger. This background has been exacerbated by Muslim frustration with their own corrupt and ineffective political, economic, and social systems. All of this has resulted in a vulnerable population ripe with anger, humiliation, and disenfranchisement. Bin Laden carefully crafted his narrative to convince Muslims that their religion and way of life are under attack by America and that a defensive war is necessary to save their way of life and regain the glory of past Islamic empires. He rooted his narrative in six points in his 1996 *Declaration of jihad against the United States*:

1. The U.S. military and civilian presence in the Prophet's homeland on the Arabian Peninsula.
2. Washington's protection and support for tyrannical Muslim governments.
3. Washington's unquestioning and unqualified support for Israel.
4. Washington's support for countries that oppress Muslims, especially Russia, China, and India.
5. U.S. and Western exploitation of Muslim energy resources at below-market prices.
6. The U.S. military presence in the Muslim world outside the Arab Peninsula.[9]

Post-9/11 actions, inactions, rhetoric, steps, and missteps by the United States have been exploited by Al Qaeda to drum up support within the Muslim world, but do not provide the full picture of the Islamic world view. The country must understand the conditions and emotions that allow Al Qaeda's ideology to find support within the Muslim world. All too often, this deeper contextual understanding is lost and discussions revert back to solutions for post-9/11 rallying cries such as the invasions of Iraq and Afghanistan. The 9/11 Commission Report shares this concern and cautions against letting "vagueness blur the strategy."[10] Unfortunately, the country has been vague and the strategy blurred. At the same time, the Muslim world shares an often misunderstood, and not homogeneous, perception of the western world and the United States. This misperception is fueled by Al Qaeda's narrative and allows their militant Islamist ideology to find support. The next section will describe this ideology.

The Ideology Behind the Name

"It is imperative to distinguish between Islam, a major world religion, and Islamism, a modern religiously based ideology that has political ends and whose extreme followers often engage in violence."[11] The ideological nature of this war has been well recognized by Al Qaeda's leadership and is clearly demonstrated in the effort they put towards their information

---

[9] Usama bin Laden, "Declaration of jihad against the United States," Al-Islah (Internet), September 2, 1996. As analyzed in Michael Scheuer, *Osama bin Laden* (New York: Oxford University Press, 2011), 113.

[10] National Commission on Terrorist Attacks upon the United States, 362.

[11] Angel Rabasa, "Where are we in the 'War of Ideas'?," in *The Long Shadow of 9/11*, ed. Brian Jenkins and John Godges (Santa Monica: RAND Corporation, 2011), 62.

operations and the mastery with which they carry them out. Ayman al-Zawahiri wrote a letter to Abu Musab al-Zarqawi to expound on this saying, "we are in a media battle in a race for the hearts and minds of our Umma. And that however far our [military] capabilities reach, they will never be equal to one thousandth of the capabilities of the kingdom of Satan [the U.S.] that is waging war on us."[12] This recognition and embrace of the idea that this is a war of ideas and that a key battlefield is the global media has given Al Qaeda a distinct advantage.

"It is not a position with which Americans can bargain or negotiate. With it there is no common ground–not even respect for life–on which to begin dialogue. It can only be destroyed or utterly isolated."[13] This relates to two pieces of the recommended approach to Al Qaeda that will be addressed in Chapter 4. First, it recognizes that there is a portion of Islamists, including most of Al Qaeda, who will never reconcile their views with the greater Muslim population. They will need to be removed from the environment through direct means in capture or kill operations. The second part speaks to the target of indirect approaches. The same spectrum of militant Islamists who will never reconcile should not be the target of indirect approaches. Nor should those efforts start with those who are most susceptible to suasion by the violent extremist ideology. The indirect efforts should start at the other end of the spectrum with American Muslims and those international Muslim scholars and political leaders who have demonstrated the greatest likeliness to denounce the militant Islamist ideology.

Al Qaeda, Islam and Islamism – Where are the Lines Drawn?

"Our enemy is twofold: Al Qaeda, a stateless network of terrorists that struck us on 9/11; and a radical ideological movement in the Islamic world, inspired in part by Al Qaeda, which has

---

[12] Ayman al-Zawahiri to Abu Musab al-Zarqawi, Letter on July 9, 2005 (accessed on February 21, 2012 from http://patriotpost.us/reference/zawahiri-letter/).
[13] National Commission on Terrorist Attacks upon the United States, 362.

spawned terrorist groups and violence across the globe." [14] While Al Qaeda is partially

weakened, "the [ideology] is gathering, and will menace Americans and American interest long

after Usama bin Laden and his cohorts are killed or captured."[15] Written many years before bin

Laden was in fact killed, the commission seems to have been quite accurate in their assessment

that his death would not mean the end to Al Qaeda. "Our strategy must match our means to two

ends: dismantling the Al Qaeda Network and prevailing in the longer term over the ideology that

gives rise to Islamist terrorism."[16] The 9/11 Commission made this explicit by identifying the

source of the danger as "Islamist terrorism – especially the Al Qaeda network, its affiliates, and

its ideology."[17] The commission's report goes on to say, "bin Laden and other Islamist terrorist

leaders draw on a long tradition of extreme intolerance within a minority stream of Islam . . . it is

further fed by grievances stressed by bin Laden and widely felt throughout the Muslim world."[18]

The graphic below, from *Al Qaeda's Operating Environments*, depicts the geographic

spread of the Al Qaeda Network's core elements. It would be impossible to establish long term

control over even these areas, much less all of the areas around the world in which Al Qaeda

operates or finds safe haven. This reinforces the concept that the U.S. must move away from a

kinetic "counterterrorism" approach as its main effort in the fight against Al Qaeda. Chapter 4

will expand on how the current approach should be modified.

---

[14] Ibid., 363.
[15] Ibid.
[16] Ibid.
[17] Ibid.
[18] Ibid.

Al Qaeda's ideology is directly drawn from recent theorists such as Sayyid Qutb and Abu

Bakr Naji, and indirectly founded on the writing of past writers such as Ibn Tamiyyah. Ibn

Tamiyyah, an Islamic theorist of the 14th century, wrote about *jihad* as a struggle in the name of

God that he claimed was more important than conducting a pilgrimage to Mecca. He applied

this idea to a *fatwa*, religious edict, calling upon Muslims to defend against the Mongol invasion

in the late 13th and early 14th century. His writings have been the subject of significant debate

and varied interpretations. Supporters of militant Islamism take his writings literally and apply

the same ideas to the current environment. Other scholars, religious leaders, and political leaders

advocate a different interpretation.[20] They believe that his writings were specific, and

---

[20] For more information on these conflicting interpretations, see URL: http://www.mardin-fatwa.com/about.php.

appropriate, to their time period, but do not mean that all Muslims today must participate in a *jihad* against perceived enemies of Islam, be they Muslims or non-Muslims. One of the more recent influences on Al Qaeda, who uses the extremist interpretation of Ibn Tammiyah's works, is Abu Bakr Naji, who in 2004 wrote *Management of Savagery: The Most Critical Stage Through Which the Umma will Pass*.[21] This work, only published online, describes the ideology and its purpose as harnessing the emotions and frustrations described previously to fight a prolonged war of attrition to defeat America and its allies.

One of the most important writers advocating Islamism was Sayyid Qutb. An Egyptian who was subject to harassment and imprisonment during his life, he joined the Muslim Brotherhood which opposed the pro-western government. Following the coup in 1952, Qutb quickly lost hope that Egypt would establish an Islamist-based government when Gamal Abdel Nasser established a secular government. During his persecution and imprisonment, Qutb wrote a number of works including *Milestones*, which described his version of political Islam. He advocated violence and justified terrorism against non-Muslims and apostates in an effort to bring about the reign of God.[22] His ideas have been incorporated in a school of thought called Qutbism which advocates:

- A belief that Muslims have deviated from true Islam and must return to "pure Islam" as originally practiced during the time of the Prophet.
- The path to "pure Islam" is only through a literal and strict interpretation of the Qur'an and Hadith, along with implementation of the Prophet's commands.
- Muslims should interpret the original sources individually without being bound to follow the interpretations of Islamic scholars.

---

[21] Abu Bakr Naji, "Management of Savagery: The Most Critical Stage Through Which the Umma will Pass," trans. William McCants, (accessed on February 21, 2012 from http://www.wcfia.harvard.edu/olin/images/Management%20of%20Savagery%20-%2005-23-2006.pdf).
[22] Sayyid Qutb, "Milestones," (accessed on February 21, 2012 from http://majalla.org/books/2005/qutb-milestone.pdf): 32.

- That any interpretation of the Quran from a historical, contextual perspective is a corruption, and that the majority of Islamic history and the classical jurisprudential tradition is mere sophistry.[23]

All of these theorists contributed to the ideology that eventually became militant Islamism and has become Al Qaeda's political platform. Al Qaeda's reliance on the positive reception of this ideology amongst the Muslim world, and the support or tolerance that they receive from them, makes it an important center of gravity.

Al Qaeda's Leadership

One of Al Qaeda's great strengths, and one that has set it apart from other militant Islamists organizations, is its core leadership. Al Qaeda's leadership has demonstrated an impressive resiliency since its inception. Despite concerted efforts to defeat it through attrition, Al Qaeda has been able to replace its leadership losses relatively quickly. It is an organization heavily dependent, however, on social contacts. Therefore, "people [have] become operative nodes necessary to sustain the organization -- their loss has an impact on Al Qaeda's ability to maintain funding streams, operative cells and alliances."[24] Al Qaeda has been tested many times over throughout the past decade with the loss of countless mid- and senior level leaders. It has endured all of this with little long term effect on the organizational strength of the network. In the short term, those losses have significantly disrupted its ability to plan, coordinate and conduct attacks, and lead the network, which has in turn contributed directly to the lack of major attacks on U.S. soil since 9/11. However, Al Qaeda continues to regenerate and attempts to reestablish their operational momentum.

It has been said that the U.S. "takes out the #3 man in Al Qaeda every six months", and it's not far from the truth. But to what effect? The short term disruption and destabilization is

---

[23] Dale Eikmeier, "Qutbism: An Ideology of Islamic-Fascism," *Parameters*, (Spring 2007): 87.
[24] Ward, 2.

significant. One exception to the effects that the losses have had on the Al Qaeda leadership over the long term is the quality of the replacements to fill the voids. While at the mid-level, attrition often means that less capable leaders are replaced by more capable ones; attrition at the more senior levels has had a more damaging impact. The loss of highly capable leaders such as Mohammed Atif, the operational chief of Al Qaeda at the time of his demise in 2001, and many others since then, have had a significant impact on Al Qaeda's long-term operational effectiveness. These actions have denied safe haven for the Al Qaeda leadership and have likely prevented attacks on the U.S. and its allies by denying them the opportunity to organize, coordinate and plan. However, despite these losses, in the long term the ideology lives on. New recruits are always ready to take the place of leaders and fighters who are captured or killed. This demonstrates the nature and resiliency of the organization. Further, Al Qaeda is a global cellular network with a unique form of decentralization, which is best described as flattened centralization. Its funding continues to flow from sources around the world, although counter-threat financing efforts by the Department of the Treasury and its international partners have degraded the flow. Most importantly, sanctuary still exists for Al Qaeda. It finds its primary safe haven in Pakistan where it continues to regenerate and plan offensive operations, as seen when Usama bin Laden was found in Abbottabad less than 50 miles from the capitol, Islamabad. To this extent, as well as the disruption mentioned previously, this paper in no way argues that the United States and others should stop their traditional kinetic counterterrorism activities. They are an absolutely critical part of the overall effort. However, this needs to become a supporting effort to a main effort centered on a diplomacy-based ideological confrontation. The solution to eliminating this safe haven is almost purely diplomatic, and is often made more difficult by traditional military counterterrorism activities.

Usama bin Laden and the Impact of his Loss on the Organization

Although Usama bin Laden is not the focus of this paper, no discussion of Al Qaeda is complete without considering his impact, and now the impact of his loss, on the organization. His death will undoubtedly have a significant effect on the organization, however it remains to be seen what the long term effect of his loss will be. Ayman al-Zawahiri has replaced him in title, but it is unclear whether or not al-Zawahiri, or any other senior member of Al Qaeda, can truly replicate what bin Laden meant to the global network. Bin Laden was an impressively charismatic leader, and despite his extremist outlook, was well educated in civilized society before establishing Al Qaeda. He enhanced his charismatic persona by deliberately modeling his life after that of Mohammed, the Islamic prophet.[25] The irony of bin Laden is that he established his reputation, and developed his ideas about fighting western interventions, or western presence in Islamic lands, while fighting in Afghanistan -- a war the Soviets would likely have won if the mujahedin had not been supported by the United States. He was an efficient organizer, manager, and unifier, which enabled him to accomplish the complex task of motivating a highly decentralized entity and focusing their efforts. He consolidated Al Qaeda, uniting various localized factions, and focused their frustrations on the U.S.[26] He possessed a living martyr-like status that supported recruiting and earned him the loyalty of regional violent extremist movements seeking to align themselves with the Al Qaeda Network. He further solidified this loyalty though his "iron fist centralized control of the organization."[27] At the same time, he demonstrated a stroke of organizational mastery, whether by design or otherwise, in balancing centralized command with decentralized execution. This ability, charisma, and celebrity-like

---

[25] Peter Bergen, *The Longest War: The Enduring Conflict Between America and Al-Qaeda* (New York: Free Press, 2011), 25.
[26] Ibid., 24.
[27] Ibid., 25.

status made him strategically significant to Al Qaeda. It remains to be seen whether or not al-Zawahiri will be able to carry that torch for the network.

Bin Laden's importance to the network makes the study of what made him important a critical part of developing an approach to defeat the organization.

> Like many of history's most effective leaders, bin Laden tells a simple story about the world that is easy to grasp, even for those of his followers from Jakarta to London who have not had a chance to sit at his feet. In bin Laden's telling, there is a global conspiracy by the West and its puppet allies in the Muslim world to destroy true Islam, a conspiracy that is led by the United States. This single narrative purports to explain all the problems of the Muslim world.[28]

He never held the religious credentials supposedly required to issue his various *fatwas* and other declarations. What he shared with the likes of Adolf Hitler was the ability to understand and exploit the emotions of a society that felt itself wronged in order to enflame their passions. He developed a narrative that explained in detail how "U.S. foreign policy in the Muslim world was the reason al-Qaeda is attacking America."[29] He twisted the realities of history, as well as contemporary issues such as the long running war between Russia and Chechnya, to fit the needs of his narrative. As noted authority Peter Bergen said, "he [was] never one to let facts get in the way of his narrative of American-led Muslim humiliation."[30] Although they occurred over a decade after he created Al Qaeda, the wars in Iraq and Afghanistan gave him quite a bit of material to work with and provided examples of how he effectively altered the beliefs of a large portion of the Muslim population. For example, he claimed that the U.S. attack on Iraq and Saddam Hussein "wasn't because he was flouting UN resolutions . . . but rather a plot by America to take over a great Arab nation."[31] His various writings and speeches demonstrate the development of his narrative. "What he has condemned the United States for is simple–its

---

[28] Ibid., 26.
[29] Ibid., 27.
[30] Ibid.
[31] Ibid., 26.

policies in the Middle East: its wars in Iraq and Afghanistan; its support for regimes, such as Egypt and Saudi Arabia, that bin Laden regards as apostates from Islam; and its support for Israel."[32] Despite obvious flaws in his logic, it becomes quickly obvious to anyone who objectively analyzes his writings that he is misinterpreting facts in order to support his argument. Regardless, his message is well received, both amongst radicalized supporters and even amongst more moderate Muslims, who find themselves identifying with his narrative even if they do not become active supporters. His recognition of this strong narrative, true or not, and the ideology that went along with it, as the center of gravity for Al Qaeda was critical. His ability to establish and maintain that narrative for over twenty years was also critical to the organization's success. This fact speaks to the real importance of bin Laden to the network. He was a larger than life ideologue who was able to convince large portions of the Muslim world to believe in his narrative and thus to support, tacitly if not actively, Al Qaeda and its associated movements.

Ayman al-Zawahiri, previously Al Qaeda's number two man and a principle advisor, has now assumed leadership of the network following bin Laden's death. Described by many as the brains of the operation, he has the intellect and religious credentials that bin Laden lacked. Al-Zawahiri came to Al Qaeda from the Egyptian Islamic Jihad where, as the leader, he focused his efforts domestically on one of the repressive regimes that were fueling Muslim anger at the time. In 1998 he merged his organization with Al Qaeda and assumed a leadership position within the network that he then used to try to influence bin Laden to focus his efforts within the Islamic world first, before focusing on the U.S. However, bin Laden maintained that attacking the U.S. first would end its support for what he called "apostate regimes" in the Islamic world, thus dooming them to a quick demise. Through 2011, al-Zawahiri's counsel and religious credibility were important to Al Qaeda. However, as the head of the organization, it remains to be seen

---

[32] Ibid., 27.

21

whether or not he will have the same charisma and strength of personality that his predecessor had. Bin Laden's personality and understanding of the nature of his position as the symbolic head of the violent extremist ideology was critical to the network's survival and growth. It is unclear whether or not al-Zawahiri will be able to match bin Laden's mastery of information and propaganda in support of his narrative.

On the surface, it is this narrative that the United States must counter in order to defeat Al Qaeda. However, that would entail some version of a public debate in which the voice of the western world could be heard, and more importantly listened to objectively. The western world lacks the legitimacy, in the eyes of the Muslim world, to engage in this kind of a direct debate and Usama bin Laden knew that. He exploited his propaganda advantage of unfettered access to the Muslim population, knowing that any direct counter from a western leader, political or religious, would be discounted as biased and false. He enhanced his advantage by quieting the only segment of the population that could have countered his narrative directly: the Muslim population itself. By drawing a link between the "evils" of the *kafirs* in the western world and the Muslims that supported them, he made it extremely difficult for mainstream Muslims to address the inconsistencies and misinterpretations in his communiqués.

Al Qaeda's Goals and Their Use of Violence to Achieve Them

Al Qaeda's long term goal is to reestablish the caliphate to its historic apex of Islamic power. While the term caliphate, in historical context, refers to the geographic spread of the old Islamic empires and, most recently, the Ottoman Empire, Al Qaeda uses it to mean a global empire founded on an Islamist ideology. In the short term, this would require remerging religious and political power under the same authority and ejecting secular governments and all western/non-Islamic influences from existing Islamic countries.[33] Like many (but not

necessarily all) Islamist groups, Al Qaeda uses violence, or terrorism, as a means of obtaining its

goals. Many organizations use terrorism, including drug cartels, international criminal

syndicates, and even some governments. Terrorism does define the organization; it is a means to

an end. Al Qaeda uses terrorism to achieve the ends described above. The slide below was used

by General Abizaid, the Commander of U.S. Central Command at the time, during testimony to

the Senate Armed Services Committee regarding the short and long term goals of militant

Islamism as espoused by Al Qaeda and its associated movements.

---

[33] Ward, 5.

Figure 1. Slide used by General Abizaid during briefing to Congress[34]

Al Qaeda is a global insurgency trying to achieve a political end: to establish a caliphate by first gaining control of the area covered by the old Islamic Empires, most recently the Ottoman Empire, and second by expanding their Islamist rule to encompass the entire world. As shown, Al Qaeda is an insurgency and must be treated as such.

The Future of the Al Qaeda Network

Al Qaeda has evolved and will continue to do so as the nature of the environment in which it lives changes. Already its leadership losses have forced them to change significantly. It

---

has become more decentralized as senior leaders, most recently Usama bin Laden, have been removed from the network. Its freedom of movement and ability to organize, train, and direct operations has been degraded as its sanctuaries have been denied due to the increased counterterrorism operations of the United States and its partners around the world. The Arab Spring has the potential to deal them a significant blow. Much of their narrative relies on the frustrations of Muslims living under repressive regimes that were allied with the U.S. If those regimes fall, as some of them have during the Arab Spring, and are replaced by representative governments that are responsive to the needs of their citizens it would affect their support for Al Qaeda. The loss of perceived legitimacy of one of its foundational arguments could bring into question the validity of the rest of Al Qaeda's arguments. In the short term, however, there is also an opportunity for Al Qaeda to expand its influence during a period of instability if those countries are not able to quickly establish some form of effective representational government. In the long term, if Al Qaeda is able to twist the narrative to demonstrate that it was in fact responsible for the fall of those regimes, popular support may increase. The withdrawal of U.S. forces from Iraq has the potential to remove another of Al Qaeda's grievances, but may also bolster its narrative if it is able to convince the Muslim world that it was responsible for pushing the U.S. out.

Al Qaeda Analyzed

In order to develop an appropriate comprehensive approach to Al Qaeda, it is important to highlight its strengths and weaknesses. Al Qaeda's strategic center of gravity is its ideology, which some scholars broaden to the ideology and leadership. While Usama bin Laden's death certainly disrupted the organization, it did not lead to its downfall as many had predicted it would prior to May 2011. His replacement, Ayman al-Zawahiri, and the replacements for other senior leaders, are not making the same contributions to the network that their predecessors did. Despite this, the network lives on, and is continuing its efforts to conduct attacks against the United States and its allies. Thus, the leadership of the network is a vital enabler of the ideology, but not the actual center of gravity. Al Qaeda draws its strength from several sources, all related to its ideological center of gravity. The first is the fact that, because its center of gravity is an ideology, it cannot be defeated through direct methods. The second is its decentralized and cellular structure that allows for independent operations coordinated by the central leadership towards a common purpose, fulfilling the vision of their ideology. Finally, and arguably most importantly, it draws strength from the worldwide Muslim population. This strength manifests itself in two ways: it relies heavily on the more extremist segments that provide active and direct support. It also relies on the entire Muslim population for its passive tolerance of Al Qaeda's use of their religion for violent political purposes. This is a critical source of Al Qaeda's strength and one that the United States needs to spend more time addressing. Understanding its strengths exposes Al Qaeda's weaknesses because the strengths also represent fairly significant vulnerabilities. The ideology is based on flawed interpretations of historical writings and factually limited relating of historical events. The other strength that Al Qaeda relies on, the underlying conditions within the environment that make the population more likely to support it, are able to be changed. Chapter 4 will look at how the instruments of national power can be more effectively employed to address these weaknesses in order to defeat Al Qaeda.

CHAPTER 2: COUNTERTERRORISM OR COUNTERINSURGENCY

"We are in a battle, and more than half of this battle is taking place in the battlefield of the media"[1]

> From a letter written by Ayman al-Zawahiri to Abu Musab al-Zarqawi on 9 July 2005

Defining the War Against Al Qaeda

Al Qaeda and Terrorism

"America is at war with a faith-driven force that dwarfs anything that can, with intellectual honesty, be called terrorism."[2] Terrorism is a tactic not a strategy. The word terrorism engenders "an unspecific definition of the threat that [does] not distinguish between groups with limited means and objectives . . . and groups with global reach and unlimited objectives, such as Al Qaeda, [and does] not provide an adequate framework for confronting the complex Islamist . . . threat."[3] Understanding what terrorism is will assist in accurately characterizing the network, which in turn is critical to developing a holistic approach to defeating it. The United States defines terrorism as "premeditated, politically motivated violence perpetrated against non-combatant targets by sub-national groups or clandestine agents."[4] Terrorist groups are further defined as "any group practicing, or which has significant subgroups which practice, international terrorism."[5] Obviously not a sufficient definition upon which to base a national policy, but it does identify the key element in this discussion which is that Al Qaeda's use of violence is politically motivated. This distinction runs counter to Al Qaeda's preferred self-description as religious warriors, but was true then and is still true now.

---

[1] Ayman al-Zawahiri to Abu Musab al-Zarqawi, Letter on July 9, 2005, http://patriotpost.us/reference/zawahiri-letter (accessed on February 21, 2012).

[2] National Commission on Terrorist Attacks upon the United States, *The 9/11 Commission Report: Final Report of the National Commission on Terrorist Attacks Upon on the United States,* (New York: Norton, 2004), 199.

[3] Angel Rabasa, "Where are we in the 'War of Ideas'?," In *The Long Shadow of 9/11*, ed. Brian Jenkins and John Godges (Santa Monica: RAND Corporation, 2011), 62.

[4] U.S. Code, Title 22, Section 2656f.

[5] Ibid.

After 9/11, the United States adopted the loose characterization of "the war on terrorism [as] a political necessity, it created some conceptual confusion, because terrorism is, after all, a tactic that can be employed by different groups to pursue different objectives, irrespective of ideology."[6] The 9/11 commission report defined "terrorism [as] a tactic used by individuals and organizations to kill and destroy."[7] In an effort to clarify the confusion surrounding the mischaracterization of extremist elements, the Organization for Security and Cooperation in Europe (OSCE) has developed a framework for better understanding and addressing the threat. They coined the acronym VERLT, Violent Extremism and Radicalization that Lead to Terrorism, which puts terrorism in its appropriate context. They identify the terrorism itself as an outgrowth of the extremism and radicalization, and advocate that it must be addressed from that perspective. Their perspective recognizes that it is vital to have "a better understanding of the dynamics and mechanics of Violent Extremism and Radicalization that Lead to Terrorism [which] is central to formulate and implement effective strategies to combat terrorism."[8]

The terrorism-focused approach to defeating Al Qaeda has not worked. It uses an incomplete perspective of the problem as a starting point, which results in an inadequate approach. It focuses on the symptoms, rather than the causes of the problems. Michael Scheuer writes that:

> The U.S. government assumes that it knows what we are facing in Al Qaeda and its allies: they are terrorists, roughly the same kind of state-supported terrorists we have faced since the 1970s, only there are more of them. This is not the assumption on which to operate. While it clearly is inaccurate to identify Al Qaeda as a nation-state–mostly because it has no fixed address–it is a greater and more damaging error to describe them as terrorists. [9]

---

[6] Rabasa, 62.
[7] National Commission on Terrorist Attacks upon the United States, 363.
[8] Organization for Security and Cooperation in Europe, "Secretariat – Action Against Terrorism Unit," OSCE, http://www.osce.org/atu/45995 (accessed on January 29, 2012).
[9] Michael Scheuer, *Imperial Hubris: Why the West is Losing the War on Terror* (Washington, DC: Potomac Books Inc, 2004), 198.

He goes on to argue that the U.S. will be unable to defeat Al Qaeda as long as the strategy is founded on what he calls the terrorist paradigm.[10] This paradigm leads to an enemy-centric approach that defaults to an attrition based mindset for defeating Al Qaeda. A global insurgency such as Al Qaeda must be fought "in a different manner and on a larger scale than terrorism, and wars against a competently led insurgency–and bin Laden [proved] himself far more than just competent–last longer, cost more money and lives, and are more steadily brutal than episodic confrontations with terrorists."[11] Embracing a new paradigm as a foundation for an enhanced strategy and approach towards Al Qaeda begins with an understanding of them as a global insurgency.

In both Iraq and Afghanistan, the United States, and its coalition partners, employed counterterrorist type methods to confront insurgencies in those countries. As the coalition began to realize that a comprehensive approach to the insurgency was required, it shifted its focus to a comprehensive counterinsurgency approach. This approach included traditional counterterrorism activities, such as raids to capture high level insurgent leaders, but shifted the main effort towards the population. Historically, counterinsurgencies have demonstrated that the population is the center of gravity in those types of wars and that all efforts should focus on them. Counterterrorism activities have an important place in counterinsurgencies, since removing key insurgent leaders disrupts the insurgency's ability to influence the population. However, if those counterterrorism activities are not subordinated to a larger effort, they will ultimately fail. The U.S., and the international coalition of peoples and governments against "terrorism," must adopt a similar approach to its policy to defeat Al Qaeda and its associated movements. Counterterrorism activities, including unilateral raids, forcign security forces

---

[10] Ibid.
[11] Ibid., 199.

capacity building, and others, remain critical to the effort to defeat Al Qaeda. They keep the network off balance by removing key leaders, disrupting planning and coordination, and preventing attacks; however, focusing on these efforts will not defeat the Al Qaeda Network in the long term. The main effort must be shifted to a more population-centric approach, in this case focusing on the global Muslim population, which must be convinced to isolate Al Qaeda and embrace what has been called the mainstream Muslim narrative. This narrative describes a moderate view of the religion that supports universal rights, democracy (although not necessarily American style liberal democracy), separation of religion and state, and freedom of religion.

Al Qaeda the Insurgency

Al Qaeda is a global insurgency rather than merely a "terrorist organization." David Galula, in *Counterinsurgency Warfare,* defines an insurgency as "a protracted struggle conducted methodically, step by step, in order to attain specific intermediate objectives leading finally to the overthrow of the existing world order."[12] Galula goes on to paraphrase Clausewitz saying, "Insurgency is the pursuit of the policy of a party, inside a country, by every means."[13] Al Qaeda is clearly conducting a protracted struggle to attain their intermediate political objectives, removal of the U.S. and western influence from the Middle East, and the destruction of Israel, leading to their final political objective of overthrowing the existing world order and establishing a global Caliphate. They are militant Islamists seeking a change in political power, and are clearly executing the policy of a party by every means. Galula also notes that the insurgent's "formidable asset [is] the ideological power of a cause on which to base his action."[14] Al Qaeda demonstrates this with their ability to appeal to the sympathies of the

---

[12] David Galula, *Counterinsurgency Warfare: Theory and Practice* (Connecticut: Praeger Security International, 1964), 2.
[13] Ibid., 1.
[14] Ibid., 4.

worldwide Muslim population. Its message is one of violence and aggression, characteristics supposedly shunned by the Islamic religion, yet it has found wide appeal. It speaks to the frustrations of a group of people mostly passed by the industrial and information ages, who often live under restricted freedoms, and who harken back to the age of the Ottoman Empire when the Islamic world was an internationally recognized power. Ironically, the Ottoman Empire was relatively tolerant for its time of Christians and Jews living within the Empire and even within Constantinople itself. The recent Arab Spring may change the equation with respect to many of the grievances of the disaffected Muslim population, which was repressed by totalitarian regimes supported by the U.S.

U.S. Army doctrine on counterinsurgency operations (FM 3-24), similar to Galula, defines an insurgency as "an organized, protracted politico-military struggle designed to weaken the control and legitimacy of an established government, occupying power, or other political authority while increasing insurgent control."[15] Similarly, joint doctrine (JP 3-24) states, "While each insurgency is unique and often adaptive, there are basic similarities among insurgencies; in all cases, insurgent military action is secondary and subordinate to a larger end."[16] As described previously, Al Qaeda uses violence (terrorism) to achieve its political ends, ultimately seeking a global Caliphate. Thus terrorism is a means not an end. Therefore, characterizing a war as one against "terrorism" is misleading. Al Qaeda clearly shows many similarities to four of the characteristics of insurgencies laid out in JP 3-24. An analysis of Al Qaeda in the context of these characteristics will further demonstrate the fact that it is a global insurgency.

---

[15] U.S. Department of the Army, *Counterinsurgency Operations,* Field Manual 3-24 (Washington, D.C.: Department of the Army, December 2006), 1-1.

[16] U.S. Joint Chiefs of Staff, *Counterinsurgency Operations*, Joint Publication 3-24 (Washington, D.C.: Joint Chiefs of Staff, October 5, 2009), II-2.

The first characteristic from JP 3-24 identifies one of an insurgent's ends as political change, which it states tend to be ideologically driven. [17] Al Qaeda clearly holds political change as one of their ends, and bases this change in their ideology. Usama bin Laden's objectives include expelling western influence from Muslim lands, removing apostate governments from Islamic countries, and reestablishing the Caliphate. His guidance gave the organization tangible direction as an insurgent movement for political change throughout both the Islamic world and ultimately the entire world. The second characteristic is the organization of insurgencies which JP 3-24 states are composed of a political wing and a military wing. [18] Al Qaeda uses a cellular organization which enables the existence of highly decentralized operational cells or military wings, all of which operate under the guidance of the organization's political wing, Al Qaeda Senior Leadership. The third characteristic is the approach which an insurgent group uses. [19] Al Qaeda uses a composite of two approaches identified in JP 3-24: terrorism focused activities and protracted popular war. In a terrorism focused approach, the insurgent wages terrorism through small, independent cells that require little popular support enabling them to operate in permissive, semi-permissive or even non-permissive environments. Al Qaeda, faced with effective internal security forces in most of the countries in which it operates, has adopted many characteristics of the terrorism focused approach to accomplish their ends. They also demonstrate characteristics of the protracted popular war approach which enables them to preserve their forces and reduce those of their enemies. The final characteristic is the cause which Al Qaeda uses as its rallying message. JP 3-24 states that "competent insurgents seek to establish control of the population and rally cooperation and popular support for their cause."[20]

---

[17] Ibid., II-3.
[18] Ibid., II-16.
[19] Ibid., II-20.
[20] Ibid., II-23.

The cause is a principle for which the insurgents and their supporting population are willing to fight. The strength of this cause often relies on the insurgents exploiting existing grievances within the population to further their own ends. Al Qaeda has developed a strong strategic narrative that speaks to Muslims worldwide and evokes strong emotional support for their cause. This consistent narrative has enabled them to establish wide appeal and rally popular support for their ideology in many of the Islamic countries around the world. These four characteristics of insurgencies clearly show ways in which Al Qaeda demonstrates its nature as a global insurgency.

The United States, and the international community, need to reject the simplistic paradigm of a cellular network of "terrorists" around the world who operate in a vacuum, isolated from their environments. They must acknowledge that Al Qaeda and its associated movements are waging a "popular, worldwide, and increasingly powerful insurgency."[21]

What Does Focusing on a Counterinsurgency Mean to the U.S.?

The foregoing discussion demonstrates the complexity of what must be done, and what is being done successfully in many cases. The approach being used by the United States, however, is founded in a counterterrorism attrition mentality of defeating the enemy by cooperating with international allies, or working unilaterally, to remove Al Qaeda members from the environment. Any approach that focuses the majority of its efforts on counterterrorism, as the United States currently does, will fail to defeat the network. As discussed earlier [in Chapter 1], counterterrorism operations are critical to success but will never actually defeat the Al Qaeda Network. Al Qaeda must be treated as a global insurgency. By understanding the complete characterization of the network, the nation can begin to address the real causes of the current conflict rather than simply the symptoms readily seen on the surface. Only an approach that

---

[21] Scheuer, 198.

directly and aggressively addresses these causes, and is backed by a clear national policy and strategy, can have a chance of defeating Al Qaeda. It must be part of an international ideological confrontation that aggressively engages the Muslim population in deliberate discourse with the intent of building a critical mass of moderate Muslims from within that will sustain a Muslim-focused and western enabled effort to alienate and defeat Al Qaeda and its associated movements.

CHAPTER 3: CASE STUDIES -

THE COLD WAR, THE CUBAN MISSILE CRISIS, AND CJTF-HOA

There are several historical examples that provide insight into improved approaches to defeating Al Qaeda. As shown in the previous chapters, this is primarily an ideological conflict, requiring a mostly indirect and non-kinetic approach, which is currently being addressed through a military main effort. This chapter will examine the Cold War; a superpower on superpower struggle between nation states. At its basic level, however, it was an ideological confrontation between communism and democracy, with parallels to the ideological confrontation that the U.S. faces today with Al Qaeda and militant Islamism. Next, the paper will analyze the Cuban Missile Crisis demonstrating the effectiveness of aggressive, hard-line diplomacy. This is one of the most important lessons that must be applied to the future approach to counter Al Qaeda. Finally, at the other end of the spectrum, the last case study will be the stand-up and ongoing operations of Combined Joint Task Force – Horn of Africa (CJTF-HOA). It is an interagency headquarters that operates in 10 countries, and works with 11 other countries, in eastern Africa that demonstrate many of the conditions identified as conducive to the growth of violent extremist organizations.[1] CJTF-HOA has focused on a non-kinetic, whole of government, approach which has been quite successful. Each case study will provide a brief overview of the background and similarities to the current situation with Al Qaeda. They will be analyzed to identify the lessons pertinent to the current conflict and provide a brief description of how those lessons should be applied.

---

[1] Combined Joint Task Force – Horn of Africa, "CJTF-HOA Fact Sheet," CJTF-HOA, http://www.hoa.africom.mil/pdfFiles/Fact%20Sheet.pdf (accessed February 15, 2012).

The Cold War

There is one sign the Soviets can make that would be unmistakable, that would advance dramatically the cause of freedom and peace. General Secretary Gorbachev, if you seek peace, if you seek prosperity for the Soviet Union and Eastern Europe, if you seek liberalization: Come here to this gate! Mr. Gorbachev, open this gate! Mr. Gorbachev, tear down this wall!

Perhaps this gets to the root of the matter, to the most fundamental distinction of all between East and West. The totalitarian world produces backwardness because it does such violence to the spirit, thwarting the human impulse to create, to enjoy, to worship.[2]

President Reagan: Remarks on East-West relations
at the Brandenburg Gate in West Berlin

Background

The Cold War is the most well known of these three case studies and provides several

useful parallels for the effort to defeat Al Qaeda and demonstrates several lessons which can be

applied to a new approach against them. As a superpower on superpower confrontation, the

Cold War initially appears to be at the opposite end of the conflict spectrum from the United

States' confrontation with Al Qaeda. However, at its basic level it was an ideological

confrontation between western democracy and communism, each desiring to spread their

ideology throughout the world. Similarly, Al Qaeda is attempting to spread their militant

Islamist ideology throughout the world today. Communism was countered through the concerted

application of all instruments of U.S. national power, eventually leading to the defeat of the

communist ideology and its replacement with a democratic ideology.

---

[2] President Ronald Reagan, "Speech at the Brandenburg Gate" (Presidential address, Berlin, Germany, June 12, 1987).

Approaching the Ideological Confrontation

The Islamic Radical threat of this century greatly resembles the bankrupt ideology of the last . . . In many ways, this fight resembles the struggle against communism in the last century.[3]

President George W. Bush, October 6, 2005

The Cold War was a time of ideas and leadership. Senior leaders took hard and consistent stances, and stuck to those positions. In the current conflict, leaders are often unsure of how to best deal with the sensitive topic of a political ideology linked with a religion whose population is overwhelmingly distrustful of the U.S. Much has been made of contemporary and historic Islamic writers and thinkers whose works have been used, or misused through misinterpretation for their purposes by Al Qaeda and its associated movements. Historical Islamic theorists such as Ibn Tamiyyah, an Islamic theologian who wrote in the 11th and 12th centuries, are often cited in Al Qaeda's communiqués, and more often than not are taken out of context or with complete disregard for the original writers' intent. As shown previously, the western world does not need to debate the veracity of those interpretations. They have been debunked by both western and, more importantly, contemporary Islamic scholars, theologians and religious leaders. A battle of logic and reason between a westerner and Al Qaeda's leadership would obviously be a wasted effort; however, the U.S. must draw a firm and clear line in the sand, and then aggressively encourage and enable the voices of mainstream Islam to discredit Al Qaeda and its associated movements, and ultimately to take back their religion. Direct confrontation with the Soviet Union occurred sporadically through proxies and had little effect on the eventual outcome of the Cold War, with the possible exception of Afghanistan. The real battle took place in the ideological realm. Ideologically, the U.S. drew a line in the sand

---

[3] President George Bush, "Speech at the National Endowment for Democracy" (Presidential address, Washington, D.C., October 6, 2005).

against communism, established a clear national policy and strategy, and aggressively supported those who had the credibility to speak about it. These were former citizens of communist states and those who continued to live under the communist yoke, but had the courage to stand up for what they thought was right, at great risk to themselves and their families. The U.S. began the war against Al Qaeda with this kind of line in the sand when President Bush said, "Either you are with us or you are with the terrorists," during a speech to the nation on September 20, 2001.[4] Unfortunately, this hard line became diluted over time as good intentions mistakenly led national leadership to soften this message. The U.S. must do this again by resuming this hard edged diplomacy, and encouraging and enabling credible voices of the Muslim community.

Throughout the ideological confrontation, the Soviets engaged in worldwide activities with a heavy handed ideology, which was unsuccessful over the long term. It was starkly contrasted with American values through an ideology based global engagement strategy. American public diplomacy and development had a strong message of American values behind every action or message. Today's engagement efforts lack the strong message of aggressively advocating a moderate ideology. Many government organizations are actively engaged with susceptible Muslim communities around the world. However, these engagement activities serve more of a "show the flag" function than their Cold War predecessors. Cold War diplomacy had an edge to it that ensured an aggressive and unflinching advocacy of western values. President Reagan spoke about the effectiveness of his speech at the Brandenburg Gate cited at the beginning of this section:

> There are a couple of sentences in this speech about tearing down the wall and opening the gate that I like quite a bit, and it actually makes the speech. I'm told that the State Department and the National Security Council thought the lines were too provocative. Just because our relationship with the Soviet Union is

---

[4] President George Bush, "Speech to a joint session of Congress" (Presidential address, Washington, D.C., September 20, 2001).

improving doesn't mean we have to begin denying the truth. That is what got us into such a weak position with the Soviet Union in the first place. The line stayed and got quite a reaction from the crowd.[5]

President Reagan talking about his Berlin Wall speech, June 12, 1987

In the future the U.S. must recognize the importance of strong messages and the effect that they have on the intended audiences. Strong messages will always evoke strong reactions, but the U.S. should carefully observe the source of those reactions. Extremist groups will always respond strongly to any message from the U.S. The U.S. must target their messages to the intended audience, the mainstream Muslim population, and ensure that they understand the strength and commitment behind America's message.

Building Organizations to Defeat Ideas

Throughout the Cold War, the U.S. built effective organizations to support the effort to defeat the communist ideology that were critical to the end result. The United States Information Agency was established in 1953 by President Eisenhower with the mission to "understand, inform and influence foreign publics in promotion of the national interest, and to broaden the dialogue between Americans and U.S. institutions, and their counterparts abroad."[6] It was responsible for coordinating U.S. international information activities and programs. At the time, it was the biggest organization in the world focused solely on information activities and foreign public relations. It spent over two billion dollars per year to spread America's ideological message in 150 different countries to counter the communist message.[7] One of its goals was to "explain and advocate U.S. policies in terms that are credible and meaningful in foreign

---

[5] President Ronald Reagan, "Comments by President Reagan regarding a speech he made the same day at the Brandenburg Gate in West Germany on June 12, 1987" (accessed from http://www.reaganfoundation.org on January 3, 2012).

[6] U.S. Information Agency, "USIA Fact Sheet," USIA, http://dosfan.lib.uic.edu/usia/usiahome/factshe.htm (accessed February 15, 2012).

[7] Ibid.

cultures."[8] USIA served a critical role in communicating the country's message to the world as part of the effort to defeat communism. Another critical organization developed during the Cold War was the United States Agency for International Development. USAID grew out of the Marshall plan that was started following World War II to "stabilize a post-war Europe by providing financial and technical assistance through the European Recovery Act of 1947."[9] The success of the plan led President Kennedy to establish USAID in 1961 after recognizing the importance of creating a robust development capability to support U.S. national interests and foreign policy. His vision was an organization that would consolidate the country's development efforts in order to influence foreign populations and to prevent conflict by stabilizing third world countries. He felt that "widespread poverty and chaos lead to a collapse of existing political and social structures which would inevitably invite the advance of totalitarianism into every weak and unstable area."[10] In the current environment, totalitarianism could easily be replaced with violent extremism. USAID grew into a 15,000 person agency supporting U.S. foreign policy around the world.[11] However, the agency was cut significantly following the Cold War down to 3,000 permanent staff and now has less than 2,000 foreign service officers to support worldwide operations.[12] Both of these organizations represented indirect approaches to defeating communist ideology that were critical to its eventual demise. The effort to defeat Al Qaeda requires similar capabilities within the U.S. government.

---

[8] Ibid.

[9] Ibid.

[10] President John F. Kennedy, "Special Message to Congress on Foreign Aid" (Presidential address, Washington, D.C., March 22, 1961.

[11] Robert Gates, "Speech during Landon Lecture" (Speech, Kansas State University, Manhattan, KA, November 26, 2007).

[12] Robert Gates speech, November 26, 2007; Andrew Natsios, "Testimony to the Senate Foreign Relations Committee on April 1, 2009," http://www.foreign.senate.gov/imo/media/doc/NatsiosTestimony090401a1.pdf (accessed on January 25, 2012).

Lessons from the Cold War

One of the most important lessons from the Cold War was the understanding that the "conflict would play out as much in hearts and minds as it would on any battlefield."[13] The U.S. leadership recognized that the Cold War was not going to be won in the Fulda Gap, or even in the proxy battles that took place all over the world between the two superpowers. They believed that it would be won in the ideological confrontation that convinced first the free world of the value of democracy and capitalism, second the Soviet satellites, and finally the population and leadership of the Soviet Union. The Cold War lasted almost fifty years, indicating that defeating an ideology takes time. The U.S. must understand that the effort to defeat Al Qaeda will not be a quick one, and that expectations for a quick victory, or constant shifts in approaches due to impatience, are counterproductive. The Cold War confrontation also shows that the focus throughout all lines of effort to defeat Al Qaeda must remain the ideology, and that all other efforts are secondary or supporting. Finally, the Cold War demonstrated the critical importance of robust organizations like USAID and USIA.

While there are positive lessons from the Cold War, there are also negative lessons whose mistakes continue to be repeated. There were many examples of strong diplomacy throughout the Cold War, but the United States simultaneously "developed an over-reliance on military power, in contrast to diplomacy, to achieve its foreign policy aims" during this period.[14] This over reliance has continued to plague U.S. foreign policy throughout the conflict with Al Qaeda and pervades the current approach to defeating them. Selecting the military as the primary instrument of national power to defeat what appears to be a problem of violence ignores the true nature and depth of the problem. The symptoms of the problem are the terrorist activities carried

---

[13] Robert Gates speech, November 26, 2007.
[14] Andrew Bacevich, interviewed by Bill Moyer, September 26, 2008, Public Broadcasating Service, http://www.pbs.org/moyers/journal/09262008/transcript1.html (accessed on January 15, 2012).

out by Al Qaeda and its associated movements. A purely counterterrorism approach, focusing solely on disrupting the violence itself, would appropriately focus its efforts on military activities. However, recognizing Al Qaeda's vulnerability as its militant Islamist ideology that employs that violence to achieve political ends leads to a different approach. The U.S. must recognize that there is a "limited utility of violence as a tool of [true] statecraft."[15] The Cold War "scar" of over reliance on the military in foreign policy must be overcome in order to focus on diplomatic and development based approaches to resolve the deeper challenges.

The Cuban Missile Crisis

Background

The Cuban Missile Crisis, one of the most tense confrontations between the U.S. and the Soviet Union, is a good example of the use of aggressive and hard line diplomacy. On 1 January 1959, Fidel Castro assumed power after the Cuban Revolution, and he aligned himself with the Soviet Union and their policies in December 1960. In an attempt to trigger a rebellion to overthrow Castro, the U.S. backed a failed invasion at the Bay of Pigs in April 1961. This was followed later that summer by a buildup of Soviet ballistic missiles in Cuba, which led to a growing belief within the U.S. government that the Soviets were establishing a nuclear missile capability there. The missile crisis began in earnest on 14 October 1962 when a U-2 reconnaissance flight obtained photographic evidence that Soviet Medium Range Ballistic Missiles (SS-4 missiles with a 1000 mile range) were being assembled in Cuba.[16] A later flight on the 17 October escalated the situation further when it discovered Intermediate Range Ballistic Missiles (SS-5 missiles with a 2,200 mile range) which had the capability of hitting any city on

---

[15] Andrew Bacevich, "Speech to Massachusetts Institute of Technology - Center for International Studies" (Speech, MIT, Boston, MA, September 14, 2010).

[16] Oracle Think Quest Education Foundation, "Cuban Missile Crisis Timeline," Oracle Think Quest Education Foundation, http://library.thinkquest.org/11046/days/timeline.html (accessed on February 15, 2012).

the east coast.[17] Once President Kennedy was informed of the confirmation, he gathered his diplomatic and military advisors to begin discussions on how to address the situation. The diplomatic engagement, concerning the missiles, between the U.S. and the Soviets began on 18 October with a meeting between Kennedy and the Soviet Foreign Minister Andrei Gromyko during which Gromyko assured the President that the military aid to Cuba was purely defensive.[18] This meeting began the diplomatic interaction that continued throughout the crisis and was responsible for its resolution. The military involvement in the missile crisis began on 20 October when Kennedy ordered a defensive quarantine.[19] At that time, Kennedy and his advisors were unsure of their eventual stance, but identified the quarantine as a method of drawing a "line in the sand" and making an initial, tentative, and incomplete policy statement. The quarantine demonstrated resolve without necessitating a direct confrontation. The situation escalated on 21 October, when reconnaissance photographs showed Soviet fighters and cruise missiles on Cuba's north shore, which increased pressure on the President to respond.

Aggressive Diplomacy

The day after receiving the new reconnaissance photos, the President established his national policy in a televised speech to the nation, knowing that it would also serve the dual purpose of communicating a strong message to the Soviets. "Within the past week, unmistakable evidence has established the fact that a series of offensive missile sites is now in preparation on that imprisoned island. The purpose of these bases can be none other than to provide a nuclear strike capability against the Western Hemisphere."[20] He began the speech clearly stating what the situation was and what the Soviet intent was. His language was clear, concise, and

[17] Ibid.
[18] Ibid.
[19] Ibid.
[20] President John F. Kennedy, "Radio and Television Report to the American People on the Soviet Arms Buildup in Cuba" (Presidential address, Washington, D.C., October 22, 1962).

43

unambiguous. He made no attempt to downplay the danger in an attempt to deescalate the situation by mislabeling it as something other than what it was. "Additional sites not yet completed appear to be designed for intermediate range ballistic missiles–capable of traveling more than twice as far–and thus capable of striking most of the major cities in the Western Hemisphere, ranging as far north as Hudson Bay, Canada, and as far south as Lima, Peru."[21] He subtly pointed out that the threat was not just a threat to the U.S., but a threat to all countries of the "free world." He continued, making it clear that their actions were unacceptable. He removed any argument for rationalization or opportunity for sympathetic Americans, or the international community, to rationalize the Soviets' actions as acceptable for any reason. Kennedy went on to describe the statements made by Soviet leadership that were in stark contrast to reality. However, he did not discuss their actions from the Soviet perspective, which had the potential to lend legitimacy to the Soviet line of thinking. The Soviets were continuing their buildup and making false explanations for their actions in order to hide their real intentions until it was too late. Rather than trying to debate the veracity of their statements in the context of their intentions, Kennedy made it clear to the Soviet leadership that their actions were unacceptable and also made it clear to the American people that their intentions represented a significant threat. "Neither the United States of America, nor the world community of nations, can tolerate deliberate deception and offensive threats on the part of any nation, large or small."[22] He once again made clear that the actions were unacceptable and could not be rationalized or allowed to become the new status quo. He drew a hard line in the sand and told the American people, as well as the rest of the world, why he was right and why they should support his position.

---

[21] Ibid.
[22] Ibid.

In the rest of the speech, he reinforced the case for why their actions were not acceptable. He made it clear that their justifications were invalid and he ignored them, making it implicitly clear throughout the speech. He did not identify their justifications and debate each point. He did not approach the argument that he made in his speech from the perspective that it was anything other than the moral high ground. Countless others, media and world leaders on both sides, would argue those points and Kennedy knew that. While closely studying the Soviet and Cuban perspective, justifications, and intentions privately, and incorporating them in his decision making, he was careful to avoid touching on those in his speech. Addressing those perspectives in his speech would have lent credibility to the debate and to the Soviet position, which would have opened the door for a debate on the United States' position. By not addressing their position in his speech, he communicated very clearly to anyone listening that the Soviet Union's position was unacceptable. Kennedy then spoke clearly and decisively about the United States' policy regarding the Soviet buildup. He addressed Soviet, domestic, and international audiences. He was clear about what he expected of both the Soviets and international organizations, making it an international problem instead of just a U.S.-Soviet problem. Finally, he gave Chairman Khrushchev a way to back out of the situation, while maintaining his "party line." He closed the speech by extending an olive branch to the Soviets without compromising his critical requirements nor limiting his response options.[23]

Lessons from the Cuban Missile Crisis

The lessons from the Cuban Missile Crisis are similar to those from the Cold War in many ways; however, the Cuban Missile Crisis provides a great example as a microcosm of high

---

[23] For more on the Cuban Missile Crisis see: Robert F. Kennedy, *Thirteen Days: A Memoir of the Cuban Missile Crisis* (New York, NY: W. W. Norton and Company, 1969); and Kurt Wiersma and Ben Larson, "Fourteen Days in October: The Cuban Missile Crisis," http://library.thinkquest.org/11046/media/fourteen_days_in_october.pdf.

level diplomacy. The Kennedy administration was faced with being forced to accept a new and significantly more dangerous status quo for the United States with Soviet missiles based in Cuba. This demonstrates a parallel to the current conflict with Al Qaeda, and the Muslim world, in which the U.S. leadership often feels pressured into making conciliatory actions and statements to the Muslim world in the belief that they can win the support of Muslims in the long run. Contrary to their proclaimed grievances, Al Qaeda attacked the U.S. first. In response, there has been little condemnation of the 9/11 attacks, as well as others, from the global Muslim community. Yet the government continues to treat the issue too delicately. There are times when delicate and non-confrontational diplomacy is the appropriate approach. Some would argue that it is appropriate most of the time. The current conflict is not one of those times, and an enduring conciliatory posture is counterproductive in the long run. As it was during the Cuban Missile Crisis, the country's security is threatened. Now is the time for clear diplomacy to declare the position of the nation and to demand that American Muslims, and Muslims around the world, reject the violence that is carried out ostensibly in the name of their religion. Throughout the process, the U.S. found a way for the Soviet leadership to take actions in line with the U.S. policy while still saving face, an equally important consideration when dealing with the Muslim world.

Another key point that President Kennedy and his advisors recognized was the need for a clear understanding of the motivations behind the nation's opponents. This understanding was critical in appreciating their perspective and developing an appropriate approach. "The Soviet decision to deploy missiles in Cuba can be broken down into two categories: 1) Soviet insecurity, and 2) the fear of losing Cuba in an invasion."[24] It is clear from these comments that the

---

[24] Kurt Wiersma and Ben Larson, "Fourteen Days in October: The Cuban Missile Crisis," http://library.thinkquest.org/11046/media/fourteen_days_in_october.pdf (accessed February 15, 2012).

Kennedy administration looked beyond a default of "Soviet aggression" to truly understand Khrushchev's rationale and thought process. By addressing that deeper understanding in their approach, they were able to affect his decision making process without escalating the confrontation.

Perceptions matter: "If I had been a Cuban leader at that time, I might well have concluded that there was a great risk of U.S. invasion."[25] This statement, made by then Secretary of Defense, Robert McNamara, gives some insight into the perspective of the Cuban leadership during this period. Understanding their perceptions of potential future U.S. actions makes it easier to understand their decision to let the Soviets base nuclear capable ballistic missiles on their soil. Perceptions, and misperceptions, are responsible for much of the current tensions between the U.S. and the Muslim world. The U.S. must understand that, while statements from U.S. leadership are important and do carry weight, past actions speak louder than those words. The U.S. and western history of involvement in Muslim countries, as well as the revisionist history espoused by Al Qaeda, is an important part of the perspective with which Muslims view America today. The United States' recent history with the Muslim world includes its relationships with repressive regimes in the Middle East, in the interest of short term stability, which contrasts with country's messages of freedom, human rights, and representative government. This contrast has played heavily into current Muslim perceptions of the U.S. and is exploited by Al Qaeda in its narrative. In developing a comprehensive approach to defeating Al Qaeda, the U.S. must take into account an appreciation for the perceptions of the Muslim world and ensure that future actions match messages to the greatest extent possible.

---

[25] Ibid.

CJTF-HOA

Background

Camp Lemonnier and the Combined Joint Task Force–Horn of Africa is a contemporary example of the way ahead for the global fight against Al Qaeda and its associated movements. In fact, a good portion of that fight is already taking place with in their area of operations. CJTF-HOA was established in 2002 by USCENTCOM to conduct counterterrorism operations throughout the east African region during the early phase of Operation ENDURING FREEDOM. Over the next decade, CJTF-HOA moved ashore to Camp Lemonnier, in Djibouti, and its mission morphed from counterterrorism operations to one of "persistent engagement focused on building partner nation capacity in order to promote regional stability and prevent conflict" through a primarily indirect approach.[26] It is the only major military headquarters on the African continent and is one of two major ongoing military efforts in Africa relating to Al Qaeda and its associated movements.[27] Their current mission statement is to "conduct operations . . . to enhance partner nation capacity, promote regional security and stability, dissuade conflict, and protect U.S. and coalition interests."[28] According to GEN Ward, former commander of U.S. Africa Command, they "conduct operations to counter violent extremists throughout the region to protect U.S. and coalition interests. In cooperation with other USG departments and agencies, [they] focus operations on building regional security capacity to combat terrorism, denying safe havens, and reducing support to violent extremist organizations."[29]

---

[26] Brian Losey (Rear Admiral, former commander of CJTF-HOA), "Conflict Prevention in East Africa: The Indirect Approach," *Prism, Vol 2, No. 2* (March 2011): 77.

[27] William Ward (General, former commander USAFRICOM), "Testimony to the Senate Armed Services Committee on March 17, 2009," http://www.africom.mil/getArticle.asp?art=2816 (accessed on Februuary 7, 2012).

[28] CJTF-HOA Fact Sheet.

[29] William Ward (General, former commander USAFRICOM), "Testimony to the Senate Armed Services Committee on March 9, 2010," http://armed-services.senate.gov/statemnt/2010/03%20March/Ward%2003-09-10.pdf (accessed on Februuary 12, 2012).

CJTF-HOA operates in an environment that is well known for many of the conditions that have contributed to instability in other regions of the world and that make those regions ripe for exploitation by violent extremist organizations. CJTF-HOA has been responsible for preventing the reemergence of a transnational terrorist threat emanating from its area of responsibility. Despite its successes, CJTF-HOA has been the subject of controversy over whether or not its mission and activities, which are less kinetic than traditional military missions, would more appropriately belong to the Department of State or another agency within the U.S. government. [30] Aside from the more militarily oriented missions, such as building partner capacity, its current mission arguably could be more appropriately led by a Department of State entity with regional responsibility. Unfortunately, that capability does not currently exist within the Department of State. Additionally, they focus on individual country approaches, rather than regional approaches, and do not have the capacity to lead operations on a regional level such as CJTF-HOA. This will be a lesson learned and an issue addressed in greater detail in the next chapter.

CJTF-HOA's focus on partners and instability (a friendly network-centric approach rather than an enemy-centric approach) has enabled it to build genuine relationships with countries that are committed to addressing both domestic and regional security issues, and the root causes of the instability. They have built trust through long-term presence and a minimal footprint. They have operated on a relatively limited budget given that they have ten countries in their area of responsibility and another eleven countries surrounding that in their area of interest, and they have achieved significant effects.

---

[30] Congressional Research Service, Africa Command: U.S. Strategic Interests and the Role of the U.S. Military in Africa, July 22, 2011 (Washington, D.C.: Government Printing Office, 2011), 21.

Lines of Effort

CJTF-HOA focuses its efforts both functionally and geographically. Geographically, they are focusing on the Kenya, Ethiopia, Djibouti, and Uganda, which General Ward notes are the countries that are at the greatest risk for instability caused by extremists.[31] It is focused on a whole of government approach to build partner nation capacity in order to provide both domestic and regional security and stability, and to support and enhance effective governance in order to reduce the conditions which make populations susceptible to Al Qaeda's narrative and ideology. It is conducting an "indirect approach that focuses on populations, security capacity and basic human needs to counter violent extremism, [its] operations build and call upon enduring regional partnerships to prevent conflict. [It] conducts civil-military operations, military-to-military engagements and key leader engagements; provide enabling support; and use outreach communications to support and enable security and stability."[32] Its functional lines of effort are: military-to-military engagements, civil-military operations, strategic communications, functional engagements, key leader engagements, and coalition integration.[33] A synoptic review of some of these lines of effort follows. The military-to-military engagements focus on building the operational capacity of partner nation security forces. These engagements produce both long term benefits, increased regional capacity and independent capability, and also create the short term benefits of trained forces available to participate in the African Union Mission in Somalia (AMISOM) and the United Nations mission to Darfur. With USAFRICOM focused on capacity building activities in Kenya, Ethiopia, Djibouti, and Uganda, countries directly threatened by Al Qaeda and its associated movements, CJTF-HOA (along with Special Operations Command

---

[31] Ward Testimony, March 9, 2010.
[32] CJTF-HOA Fact Sheet.
[33] Losey, 83-87.

Africa) carries out most of those capacity building responsibilities. [34] Further, Somalia is home

to the Al Shabaab network, which aligned itself with Al Qaeda recently. The "survival of the

TFG [Transitional Federal Government] in Mogadishu depends, in large measure, on the

presence of the AMISOM and the more than 8,000 troops supplied by willing African

partners."[35] Many of those troops would not be able to carry out their missions in support of

AMISOM effectively were it not for their relationship with CJTF-HOA. For a relatively small

investment, the U.S. is able to have an effect in Somalia which is becoming more important to

regional stability as noted by the USAFRICOM commander General Ham:

> Linked to Somalia's instability is al-Qaida's dramatic increase in influence in east
> Africa over the last year. In early 2010, al-Shabaab announced their alignment
> with al-Qaida. This alliance provides al-Qaida a safe haven to plan global terror
> operations, train foreign fighters, and conduct global terror operations. This
> situation poses a direct threat to the security of the United States.[36]

Without CJTF-HOA, and parallel operations underneath Special Operations Command Africa,

the United States would be unable to contribute to security in Somalia and to support the stability

of the Transitional Federal Government. Evidence of the regional acceptance of CJTF-HOA's

mission and their success is the steadily increasing demand for these engagements as countries

recognize the positive impacts that they have had on the AMISOM troop contributing nations.[37]

CJTF-HOA's second line of effort is civil-military operations. Much of their focus for

this line of effort is targeted at the area around the Somali border, which roughly defines the

extent of violent extremist influence. The civil-military operations work closely with their host

nation counterparts to "build trust and confidence with populations vulnerable to violent

---

[34] Ward Testimony, March 9, 2010.
[35] Carter Ham (General, commander USAFRICOM), "Testimony to the Senate Armed Services Committee on April 5, 2011," http://armed-services.senate.gov/statemnt/2011/04%20April/Ham%2004-07-11.pdf (accessed on February 15, 2012).
[36] Ibid.
[37] Losey, 84.

extremist influences by providing essential services and meeting basic human needs."[38] Through

this indirect approach towards Al Qaeda and its associated movements in the East Africa region,

they have been able to help stem the spread of their ideology, mitigate instability, and minimize

the conditions that make populations susceptible to radicalization. A former CJTF-HOA

commander identified several factors that have contributed to the success of their civil-military

operations. Civil-military operations are conducted as a separate and independent line of effort

operating at locations that are selected "based on their susceptibility to violent extremist

influence and are subject to rapidly changing conditions."[39] They are coordinated with other

elements of national power and reinforced with strategic communications, and they work with

and through local partners to ensure sustainability of the programs.[40]

Strategic communications is another one of the successful lines of effort. CJTF-HOA

maximizes the effectiveness of this line by ensuring that their strategic communications are

coordinated with and directly support their other ongoing operations, and vice versa. They have

also developed a system to synchronize their communications through three levels: public and

organic means, defense support to public diplomacy, and ultimately the partner nations generate

their own messages in their local media. CJTF-HOA has maintained centralized control over

this process to ensure unity of message but has decentralized the execution significantly in order

to make it a more responsive and proactive system rather than a reactive one. To do this, they

begin with the concept that "every member on the team is a communicator."[41] They provide

training for all members of the team, and then they "ensure that that actions and words are

aligned and reflect the mutual interests and objectives of all participants," not just those of the

---

[38] Ibid., 81.
[39] Ibid., 85.
[40] Ibid., 86.
[41] Ibid.

U.S.[42] An important part of this effort are the key leader engagements that the task force conducts regularly. They have identified these engagements as an "an integral part of building enduring partnerships, [and fostering] the interaction between the [combined joint] task force and decision makers within our partner nations' militaries, governments, and religious organizations."[43]

Virtual Presence

Another important aspect of CJTF-HOA has been their ability to provide the U.S. a "virtual presence" in otherwise denied areas. CJTF-HOA trained Ugandan and Burundian troops are in Somalia as part of the AMISOM mission supporting the Transitional Federal Government (TFG). The primary contributor to insecurity in Somalia, and the primary threat to the TFG is Al-Shabaab, a violent extremist organization which has long been aligned with and supported by Al Qaeda. Ayman al-Zawahiri, the new head of Al Qaeda, and Ahmed Abdi Godane, the head of Al-Shabaab, recently announced that Al-Shabaab, known to have been loosely aligned with Al Qaeda for several years, had merged with them.[44] CJTF-HOA is critical to the United States' ability to address this new arm of Al Qaeda and to foster security and stability in Somalia. Their partners are the only method that the U.S. currently has to maintain a consistent countering presence in Somalia to ensure that Al-Shabaab is not able turn it into another Afghanistan-like safe haven for Al Qaeda. These military-to-military partnerships, with a small non-threatening presence, can enable the U.S. to address its national interests in at-risk areas, those susceptible to violent extremist organizations and instability, in the future.

---

[42] Ibid.

[43] Ibid., 87.

[44] British Broadcasting Company, "Somalia's al-Shabab Join al-Qaeda," BBC News Online, http://www.bbc.co.uk/news/world-africa-16979440 (accessed on February 10, 2012).

Defense, Diplomacy, and Development

CJTF-HOA has made great strides in interweaving the efforts of diplomacy, development, and defense in the region into a comprehensive whole of government approach. They have coordinated their military efforts with those of the country teams within their area of responsibility, and have incorporated aspects of diplomacy and development into their operations wherever possible. One former CJTF-HOA commander stated that, "engagements with East African partners are evolving beyond a whole of government approach to a more comprehensive approach where these engagements complement the capabilities and capacities of our allies, coalition partners, nongovernmental organizations (NGOs), and international organizations."[45]

CJTF-HOA's mission requires close cooperation and coordination with country teams, partner nation militaries, and host nation governments to coordinate activities. Rear Admiral Losey noted the challenges of working throughout such a diverse region as the "dynamics of the country team, the host nation, and their objectives vary considerably."[46] CJTF-HOA works closely with the country teams and partner nation governments to ensure that "activities are arranged in time, space, and purpose to achieve shared goals that support the Mission Strategic Resource Plan, USAFRICOM theater strategic objectives, and host nation objectives from inception through execution."[47] However, under the current construct, the American ambassador in each country is the authority for whole of government efforts such as these. There is no real map or existing template for this kind of relationship, despite the fact that CJTF-HOA is by no means the first regional military headquarters that has worked with embassies in multiple countries to affect regional approaches to problems. In many cases, the cooperation and focus on mutually supporting objectives and operations makes whole of government undertakings quite

---

[45] Losey, 78.
[46] Ibid., 82.
[47] Ibid.

successful. Unfortunately, the tension between an ambassador, with a country level focus, and organizations such as CJTF-HOA with a regional focus and a mission that steps broadly out of traditional military arenas into those formerly the realm of diplomats and USAID professionals, sometimes leads to challenges. The former commander also noted the importance of including host nation militaries and governments, as well as the local populations, in both the execution and the development of solutions.[48] The potential exists for external entities in these kinds of situations to examine problems from a distance, develop a solution, and then take action accordingly. CJTF-HOA's experience has proven that externally developed solutions can lead to some challenges, and that there are many benefits to incorporating both the host nation government and the local population. Both groups are far more likely to understand the history, complex relationships, and subtle nuances critical to developing a complete appreciation for the problem and then crafting an appropriate solution. Additionally, by incorporating them into the process CJTF-HOA can engender a local feeling of ownership of the solution as well as the confidence and capability to develop and implement their own independent solutions in the future.

Lessons from CJTF-HOA

There are many lessons from CJTF-HOA's example that can be applied to the effort to defeat Al Qaeda. CJTF-HOA has shown that a long term commitment, with relatively limited resources, employing a regionally focused indirect approach, that interweaves the functions of defense, diplomacy, and development, can have a significant positive impact. The CJTF-HOA headquarters has been in place for about a decade, building relationships and working closely with all of the instruments of U.S. national power as well as international partners and non-governmental organizations. Their comprehensive approach, which has also included host

---

[48] Ibid.

nation governments into the planning efforts, has been received well in Africa. CJTF-HOA has focused on a regional approach with local implementation. This has provided unifying guidance throughout eastern Africa which has made their operations against Al Qaeda far more effective. This regional approach has then been tailored at the local level to meet the unique aspects of that local environment. As mentioned above, CJTF-HOA has developed the implementation of their indirect approach along six lines of effort designed to stress a non-kinetic approach. These lines of effort, military-to-military engagements, strategic communications, civil-military operations, functional engagements, key leader engagements, and coalition integration, follow non-traditional functions for a military joint task force. They were designed to prevent conflict, eliminate the conditions that make a population susceptible to violent extremist ideology, and to bolster the ability of host nation governments and security forces to independently provide for the security and stability of their people, and they have been quite successful in doing so.

CHAPTER 4: A NEW APPROACH - STRATEGY AND IMPLEMENTATION

(DEFENSE, DIPLOMACY, AND DEVELOPMENT)

"*Otug odhguc birle ucurmez* - You cannot put out fire with flames." – Old Turkish proverb used by President Obama during a 2009 speech to the Turkish Parliament.[1]

The United States must adapt its policy for defeating Al Qaeda to reflect the characterization of the network as a global insurgency. The U.S. must also change the way it employs the tools of national power, defense, diplomacy, and development, to implement the policy. The country has become overly focused on the counterterrorism aspect of the fight against Al Qaeda, and that focus has strongly influenced the way in which the tools of national power are employed, as well as the allocation of resources in support of the fight. The "counterterrorism" approach, as used in this paper, describes an enemy-centric approach that targets Al Qaeda's leadership and their ability to employ violence. The previous chapters have demonstrated how this mischaracterization of Al Qaeda and its associated movements as terrorist organizations is inappropriate and should be replaced by a more complete and accurate description. As a global insurgency, as discussed previously, Al Qaeda can be treated as a global insurgency far more effectively than through traditional counterterrorism means. The first part of this discussion focuses on the previous and current national strategies for combating terrorism, and identifies areas in which they can be improved. An appropriately focused national strategy is critical to ensuring that the elements of national power are used effectively in the war against Al Qaeda. The chapter will then describe the current activities of the U.S. government against Al Qaeda and its associated movements in the areas of defense, diplomacy, and development. The Department of Defense, responsible for the defense portion of the approach, has long

---

[1] President Barak Obama, "Speech to the Turkish National Assembly" (Presidential address, Turkish National Assembly Complex, Ankara, Turkey, April 6, 2009).

recognized the need for a more indirect approach that favors the non-military instruments of national power. The traditional military counterterrorism efforts must continue in order to disrupt ongoing operations, but other government agencies must fill in the traditional counterinsurgency functions which are currently being ignored or under resourced. The Department of State must shift its focus from supporting the U.S. and international counterterrorism efforts to taking the lead in a whole of government counterinsurgency approach that focuses on the defeating Al Qaeda's ideology and separating them from the Muslim world. Unfortunately, they lack the capacity, either with respect to manpower or resources, to undertake many of the functions which they should be leading. USAID is leading the development function which is a critical component of this counterinsurgency approach. Unfortunately, they too lack the capacity required for the fight and are less effective than they otherwise could be. Comparing the current activities with the counterinsurgency approach identified earlier, and pulling from the lessons identified in the later case studies, the paper will recommend effective activities for each of these three areas. Finally, the activities of other organizations contributing to the war against Al Qaeda will be reviewed to provide a better understanding of the international environment in which the United States is fighting. These assessments and recommendations will support a more appropriately focused national strategy and will contribute significantly to the defeat of Al Qaeda and its associated movements.

The assessments and recommendations made in this section must be viewed from the perspective of the current domestic environment. There are significant limitations to the U.S. approach towards Al Qaeda. The debt crisis restricts the United States' (and other countries') ability to expand or even continue, diplomatic, developmental, and defense efforts. Compromises must be made to trade off less important capabilities in order to increase the capabilities of other more critical efforts. Despite the global economic situation, the United States must ask more of its partners, particularly when it comes to activities within their own borders. The U.S. may have to consider adopting an international *tache d'huile* strategy. The *tache d'huile*, or oil spot strategy, was developed during counterinsurgencies of the last century to maximize the effect of limited resources; and it may provide a model for an international strategy that focuses limited resources on Al Qaeda's critical nodes.[2]

These recommendations are partially framed by some of the principles that reoccur throughout many of the successful historical counterinsurgencies. These principles are: establishing a clear political policy, ensuring the security and safety of the population, resourcing the intense manpower requirement, eliminating the insurgency's infrastructure, patience because successful counterinsurgencies take time, and the understanding that the host nation must do the bulk of the fighting.[3] While these principles will serve as a framework or starting point for a recommended approach, there is no historical example of a global counterinsurgency. The counterinsurgency needed now will be fought country by country with a cohesive global strategy to coordinate the efforts. This makes the war against Al Qaeda and its associated movements unique in history.

National Strategy

A clear and appropriately focused national strategy towards Al Qaeda is critical to guiding and unifying the efforts of the instruments of national power to successfully defeat the network. This strategy should provide directive guidance for both the activities to be undertaken, as well as resource allocation and prioritization. As shown previously, Al Qaeda's center of

---

[2] Andrew Birtle, *U.S. Army Counterinsurgency and Contingency Operations Doctrine 1942 1976* (Washington, D.C.: Government Printing Office, 2006), 170.
[3] Paul Melshen, "Mapping Out a Counterinsurgency Campaign Plan: Critical Considerations in Counterinsurgency Campaigning," *Small Wars & Insurgencies*, 18:4, (2007), 668-673.

gravity is the support, tacit or otherwise, that it receives from within the Muslim population and the acceptance it finds for its militant Islamist ideology. A successful national strategy must focus on an indirect approach to defeat the ideology and to separate Al Qaeda from the Muslim population.

The global Muslim population is at the heart of the issues facing the United States. This is an important point that needs to be emphasized, clearly articulated, and clearly understood. The global Muslim population is not the enemy. However, as in any counterinsurgency, the population is the center of gravity. For Al Qaeda, it is a critical requirement. If they can gain and maintain the popular support of Muslims worldwide, or even intimidate or co-opt them into inaction, the United States will never be able to truly defeat them. With a favorable or tolerant population, infrastructure support, and sanctuary wherever they need it, Al Qaeda would be able to survive, continue to replenish its ranks, and eventually find a way to conduct major attacks. While several national policy and strategy documents relate to the fight against Al Qaeda, this paper focuses on the past and current national strategies for combating terrorism to demonstrate both the evolution of the strategy as well as to identify common shortfalls throughout all three. This includes identifying key elements to maintain, as well as areas in which the country's focus ought to be shifted.

The current National Security Strategy speaks in general terms about the effort to defeat Al Qaeda, appropriate for such a high level policy document. It provides effective top level guidance and leaves the more detailed description for the approach to the National Strategy for Combating Terrorism. To its credit, it describes Al Qaeda as a global network and discourages the "terrorist" moniker. While it needs to be more aggressive in its design to work with the leadership of the Muslim world to encourage them to separate Al Qaeda from the global Muslim community, it does describe the limitations of a military focused approach. However, these themes are not well translated into the National Strategies for Combating Terrorism and they are not well implemented by the whole of government. The current national strategy for combating terrorism focuses its efforts on direct approaches which most often translate to kinetic military action or at the very least the application of the military instrument of national power. These "counterterrorism" activities serve two important purposes. First, they disrupt the planning and operational activities of Al Qaeda and its associated movements in order to prevent them from conducting attacks. Second, and derived from the first, they create the time and space needed to implement the indirect actions which will lead to the downfall of Al Qaeda. These counterterrorism activities will never actually defeat these organizations; it is rather the ideological aspect that is absolutely critical to the success of this effort. As previously discussed, as long as the ideology exists, and is given credibility and recognition amongst the worldwide Muslim community, new recruits will spring up to fill the shoes of Al Qaeda leaders and operators who are either killed or captured. The nation must continue its aggressive pursuit of these organizations throughout the world in order to disrupt their operations. However, like any other counterinsurgency, this must become the secondary effort to an indirect approach that implements the recommendations made in this chapter through a whole of government approach.

The United States is not using every instrument of national power it has at its disposal. The country has defaulted to the least complicated approach; task the military to employ force against an entity threatening the safety and security of the United States and its citizens. This simplistic approach addresses the symptom not the cause, and fails to properly frame the problem facing the nation. The problem is one of two ideologies with differences based as much on misunderstandings and theological misinterpretations.

Evolution of the National Strategy Towards Al Qaeda

There have been three versions of the National Strategy for Combating Terrorism since the 9/11 attacks. The newer versions, the most recent in 2011, have altered the definitions and characterizations of the network slightly, but the approach that they direct has changed little. In reality, there has been little change in the overall approach. The first National Strategy for Combating Terrorism was written by President Bush in 2003.

2003 National Strategy for Combating Terrorism

President Bush codified the country's focus on defeating Al Qaeda and its associated movements in a national strategy that described his approach to build on the ongoing Global War on Terrorism. The first version focused on terrorism as the targeted threat. "The enemy is terrorism—premeditated, politically motivated violence perpetrated against noncombatant targets by sub-national groups or clandestine agents."[4] This language reflected the country's preoccupation with its kinetic approach to seek out members of Al Qaeda and remove them from the environment (capture or kill operations). Despite that focus, another part of this strategy demonstrated the country's growing understanding of the nature of the war it is fighting. It spoke of the "need to destroy terrorist organizations, [and] win the 'war of ideas'."[5] It began to describe an appreciation for the complexities of Al Qaeda's narrative and the conditions within the Muslim world which made it more receptive to the narrative. The strategy described Al Qaeda's dependence on the underlying conditions and the international environment that sustain their narrative, which accurately identified one of the network's key vulnerabilities: its reliance on the substandard environment [on average] within the Muslim world. It further discussed environmental conditions as being important, but did not lay out an approach to address them.

---

[4] U.S. President, *National Strategy for Combating Terrorism – 2003* (Washington, D.C.: Government Printing Office, 2003), 1.
[5] Ibid., 2.

Other sections of the strategy recognize that the network uses its narrative to develop the support it relies on from within the larger population.[6] Despite that understanding, the strategy did little to address the ideological nature of the war and it circled back to the focus of the nation's approach at the time, which was "a strategy of direct and continuous action against terrorist groups, the cumulative effect of which will initially disrupt, over time degrade, and ultimately destroy the terrorist organizations."[7] President Bush's strategy was an effective first step for the country in describing a long term approach to defeating Al Qaeda and its associated movements. His intent for a direct, enemy-centric approach is highlighted in the following statement that he made almost a year after the 9/11 attacks, "We must take the battle to the enemy, disrupt his plans and confront the worst threats before they emerge. In the world we have entered, the only path to safety is the path of action. And this nation will act."[8]

In the language he used in the strategy to describe the actions that would support his approach, he pointed towards an effect on the underlying conditions that enabled Al Qaeda's ideology to thrive.

> We will diminish the underlying conditions that terrorist seek to exploit by enlisting the international community to focus its efforts and resources on the areas most at risk. We will maintain the momentum generated in response to the September 11 attacks by working with our partners abroad and various international forums to keep combating terrorism at the forefront of the international agenda.[9]

However, the actions listed to target those underlying conditions did not differ greatly from the more direct counterterrorism activities described in his 2003 strategy. President Bush signed an updated version of his original National Strategy for Combating Terrorism in 2006, which began

---

[6] Ibid., 8.
[7] Ibid., 2.
[8] President George Bush, "Speech at the U.S. Military Academy" (Presidential address, West Point, NY, June 1, 2002).
[9] National Strategy for Combating Terrorism-2003, 12.

to lean towards a blend of direct and indirect approaches. The new strategy discussed both a

short term approach aimed at disrupting the network's ability to conduct attacks, and a long term

approach, an indirect one aimed at defeating the ideology and changing the environmental

conditions in order to defeat the network.

2006 National Strategy for Combating Terrorism

> In response to our efforts, the terrorists have adjusted, and so we must continue to refine our strategy to meet the evolving threat. Today, we face a global terrorist movement and must confront the radical ideology that justifies the use of violence against innocents in the name of religion. As laid out in this strategy, to win the War on Terror, we will . . . advance effective democracies as the long-term antidote to the ideology of terrorism.[10]

The 2006 strategy recognized that the ideological aspect was critical and in fact listed the

ideology as the first point in the way ahead. It did not go far enough to identify that action as the

main effort, or to describe, other than the advancement of democracy, how the U.S. could

accomplish that task. Further, it did not list combating the ideology in the challenges

confronting the U.S. What it did do was accurately describe the threat that the U.S. was facing at

the time.

> Our terrorist enemies exploit Islam to serve a violent political vision. Fueled by a radical ideology and a false belief that the United States is the cause of most problems affecting Muslims today, our enemies seek to expel Western power and influence from the Muslim world and establish regimes that rule according to a violent and intolerant distortion of Islam.[11]

As a result, President Bush's 2006 strategy was much better focused on the ideological aspect of

the fight, at least from an understanding of the problem. The strategy made some positive steps

identifying the war as one of both violent confrontation as well as a "battle of ideas -- a fight

---

[10] U.S. President, *National Strategy for Combating Terrorism – 2006* (Washington, D.C.: Government Printing Office, 2006), 1.

[11] Ibid., 5.

against the terrorists and their murderous ideology."[12] However, the majority of the guidance

relating to how this approach would be implemented was focused on counterterrorism activities.

The one exception to this was a "two pronged vision . . . to defeat violent extremism as a threat

to our way of life as a free and open society; and to create a global environment inhospitable to

violent extremists and all who support them."[13] In fact, his long-term approach focused on the

ideology, primarily from the standpoint of advancing democracy. It should instead focus on the

advancement of freedom, and representative government, which are better messages within the

Muslim world than that of American style democracy. Regardless, it stresses an indirect

approach that will ultimately have a much better chance at defeating Al Qaeda's center of

gravity. One critical area that the 2006 strategy addressed was the need for the Muslim

community to take ownership of the solution. This idea will be expanded on later, in the

discussion on diplomacy, but the Muslim population must stand up and isolate Al Qaeda from

the rest of the Islamic religion. President Bush's 2006 strategy described this well:

> The strategy to counter the lies behind the terrorists' ideology and deny them
> future recruits must empower the very people the terrorists most want to exploit:
> the faithful followers of Islam. We will continue to support political reforms that
> empower peaceful Muslims to practice and interpret their faith. We will work to
> undermine the ideological underpinnings of violent Islamic extremism and gain
> the support of non-violent Muslims around the world. The most vital work will
> be done within the Islamic world itself, and Jordan, Morocco, and Indonesia,
> among others, have begun to make important strides in this effort. Responsible
> Islamic leaders need to denounce an ideology that distorts and exploits Islam to
> justify the murder of innocent people and defiles a proud religion.[14]

This portion should be added verbatim to a new strategy for combating terrorism. Advocating

this message is a critical piece of the solution that needs to be implemented aggressively.

Overall, the 2006 strategy was better focused than the current strategy, which once again focused

---

[12] Ibid., 7.
[13] Ibid.
[14] Ibid., 11.

more on the direct approach rather than the indirect approach. The current national strategy for combating terrorism was written in 2011 by President Obama and does not change much from the previous two.

2011 National Strategy for Combating Terrorism

The current national strategy for combating terrorism is very much a continuation of the previous strategies. Overall it indicates a deeper appreciation for the complexities of the challenge that the country faces in its relationship with the Muslim world and Islamism specifically. However, the direction it calls for is more similar to the 2003 version than it is to the 2006 version. For example, the opening letter stresses the importance of understanding the enemy, but the rest of the document does not indicate a true understanding of Al Qaeda. It mentions the critical contributions of all the people the President feels are making a difference in the effort to defeat Al Qaeda.

> Any such strategy . . . is only as effective as the men and women charged with carrying it out. In this respect, the United States is blessed with thousands of extraordinary military, intelligence, law enforcement, homeland security, and other counterterrorism professionals who . . . help carry the fight to al-Qa'ida.[15]

Notably, it fails to mention Foreign Service officers or USAID personnel. By focusing on military, intelligence, law enforcement, and homeland security, it highlights the enemy-centric kinetic focus that is carried throughout the strategy. To defeat Al Qaeda, the country must address the conditions, narrative, and ideology that allow Al Qaeda to survive. Once those and the support that they engender are eliminated, the network will wither quickly. Counterintuitively, this requires the U.S. shift the main effort away from Al Qaeda in order to defeat them. It must be an indirect approach, while maintaining a kinetic direct approach that

---

[15] U.S. President, *National Strategy for Combating Terrorism – 2011* (Washington, D.C.: Government Printing Office, 2011), iii.

disrupts their operations allowing time and space for the indirect approach to succeed. This focus is not represented in the 2011 Strategy.

The strategy lays out four "Principles that Guide our Counterterrorism Efforts," which are: adhering to U.S. core values, building security partnerships, applying counterterrorism tools and capabilities appropriately, and building a culture of resilience.[16] While none of these are inappropriate, they could be better focused by adding reference to a focus on the countering the ideology, establishing a U.S. counter narrative, and empowering the Muslim community to establish their own narrative and to isolate Al Qaeda. Earlier in the document, it refers to "the principal focus of the National Strategy for Counterterrorism [as] the collection of groups and individuals who comprise al-Qa'ida and its affiliates and adherents."[17] The strategy goes on to say that its "focus [is] on pressuring al-Qa'ida's core while emphasizing the need to build foreign partnerships and capacity and to strengthen our resilience. At the same time, our strategy augments our focus on confronting the al-Qa'ida-linked threats that continue to emerge from beyond its core safehaven in South Asia."[18] While it is a good sign that it recognizes the need to build foreign partnerships, the strategy should be centered around an indirect approach. Phrases such as: "al-Qa'ida and its ideology has been further diminished" and "we are bringing targeted force to bear on al-Qa'ida at a time when its ideology is also under extreme pressure . . . Nevertheless, we remain keenly vigilant to the threat al-Qa'ida, its affiliates, and adherents pose to the United States," indicate that, despite what appears to be a deeper appreciation for the causes of the problem, the strategy is still rooted in an enemy-centric approach.

The "Overarching Goals" of the strategy identify eliminating safe havens, building enduring CT partnerships and capabilities, degrading links between Al Qaeda and its affiliates

---

[16] Ibid., 4.
[17] Ibid., 3.
[18] Ibid., 1.

and adherents, countering Al Qaeda ideology and its resonance, diminishing the specific drivers

of violence that Al Qaeda exploits, and depriving terrorists of their enabling means as a primary

focus. That kind of language, "eliminating, building, degrading, countering, depriving," indicate

a non-kinetic focus. However, everything seemed to be tied back to the Al Qaeda personalities

as their center of gravity rather than the ideology and the population. The overarching goals talk

about defeating the ideology a little, but the discussion concerning "Areas of Focus" and

execution do not describe how the ideology will be countered. The discussion concerning

countering Al Qaeda's ideology and its resonance says that,

> along with the majority of people across all religious and cultural traditions, we
> aim for a world in which al-Qa'ida is openly and widely rejected by all audiences
> as irrelevant to their aspirations and concerns, a world where al-Qa'ida's ideology
> does not shape perceptions of world and local events, inspire violence, or serve as
> a recruiting tool for the group or its adherents.[19]

These goals are exactly where the United States must focus. Unfortunately, the language is not

strong enough to demand support from the Muslim world nor has it driven U.S. diplomacy to do

the same. The U.S. must start being more explicit with its expectations, especially for U.S.

Muslims. This community can establish momentum within the Muslim world which they can,

through their legitimacy, spread to Muslims internationally. This more aggressive approach,

drawing clear lines of expectation, will have a greater chance of gaining some traction towards

changing the narrative in the Muslim world.

The strategy further states that "we need to pursue the ultimate defeat of al-Qa'ida and its

affiliates without acting in a way that undermines our ability to discredit its ideology."[20] They

cannot be defeated without first defeating their ideology. This is what the U.S. strategy has

backwards; the ideological confrontation is not a holding action the country fights while it

---

[19] Ibid., 10.
[20] Ibid., 7.

defeats Al Qaeda. The country needs to fight a kinetic holding action with international partners to disrupt Al Qaeda while it defeats the ideology; thus dooming Al Qaeda to defeat.

Recommended Strategy Changes

The United States must adopt a more aggressive strategy to defeat Al Qaeda that stresses an indirect approach intended to defeat their ideology and to separate them from the global Muslim population. All three of the strategies written since 9/11 reflect pieces of this, but none of them combine these tasks nor do they identify them as the country's main effort. This is not a new idea. The 9/11 Commission recommended that the strategy of the United States and its allies should have two goals: to dismantle the Al Qaeda network and to prevail in the long term over the ideology that gives rise to Islamist terrorism.[21] This is prescient, but may oversimplify the issue. The two cannot be separated, but rather go hand in hand. Al Qaeda exists because there are militant Islamists in the world who desire to unite under a common banner to further their cause through violence. They do this in the name of Al Qaeda and its associated movements. The network cannot simply be "dismantled" without first defeating the ideology that gave rise to it. If the network is addressed kinetically without successful efforts to counter the ideology, it will regenerate itself indefinitely. Kinetic efforts can disrupt the network and prevent, or at least reduce, attacks against the United States and its allies; they cannot "dismantle" the organization.

The new strategy must be aggressive, firm, and clear, but not alienating. Unfortunately, in an attempt to avoid alienating various portions of the Muslim world, U.S. strategy and diplomacy are watered down to the point that they are suboptimal. It is possible to be clear and unbending regarding expectations without necessarily alienating. This is a difficult task,

---

[21] National Commission on Terrorist Attacks upon the United States, *The 9/11 Commission Report: Final Report of the National Commission on Terrorist Attacks Upon on the United States* (New York: Norton, 2004), 363.

especially given the complexity and diversity of the countless audiences who will receive those messages, regardless of their intended recipients. However, adherence to a clear national strategy will be extremely beneficial in the long term. Secretary Rumsfeld asked the right question when he asked his advisors, "are we capturing, killing or deterring and dissuading more terrorists every day than the madrassas and the radical clerics are recruiting, training and deploying against us? Does the U.S. need to fashion a broad, integrated plan to stop the next generation of terrorists?"[22] The answer is, "yes." As the case studies showed, the new strategy should be rooted in: an indirect approach, a focus on ideology, aggressive diplomacy, and a growth in the country's capacity to perform those functions.

This new strategy will be carried out primarily through the defense, diplomacy, and development functions of government.

> The United States achieves its greatest effect when all USG agencies work collaboratively in applying the tools of diplomacy, development, and defense to meet our national security objectives. Congress can modernize our nation's approach to emergent challenges, made evident in the first decade of this new century, by supporting funding and further development of the other USG departments and agencies with whom we partner and support.[23]

The following sections will explore the contributions that each of the three functional areas are making towards defeating Al Qaeda, and make recommendations based on the previous analysis, as well as the lessons learned from the case studies, for a more effective approach within each functional area.

---

[22] Ibid., 375.
[23] William Ward (General, former commander USAFRICOM), "Testimony to the Senate Armed Services Committee on March 9, 2010," http://armed-services.senate.gov/statemnt/2010/03%20March/Ward%2003-09-10.pdf (accessed on Februuary 12, 2012).

Defense

> Where possible, what the military call kinetic operations should be subordinated to measures aimed at promoting better governance, economic programs that spur development, and efforts to address the grievances among the discontented, from whom the terrorists recruit.[24]
>
> Secretary Robert Gates

The Defense function of the effort to defeat Al Qaeda is the most mature, the most robust, the most visible, but is only a supporting effort behind diplomacy and development. Defense is described first because, as it is the most mature of the three, it carries the fewest recommended changes, and ultimately has less to do with Al Qaeda's defeat than either diplomacy or development. The Department of Defense has carried the majority of the responsibility for defeating Al Qaeda since 9/11 but there are many, particularly within DoD, who are trying to change that. Secretary of Defense Robert Gates gave a speech at Kansas State University in 2007 in which he discussed the need for a change in the country's approach based on recent lessons learned.

> One of the most important lessons of the wars in Iraq and Afghanistan [both counterinsurgencies] is that military success is not sufficient to win: economic development, institution building and the rule of law, promoting internal reconciliation, good governance, providing basic services to the people, training and equipping indigenous military and police forces, strategic communications, and more – these, along with security, are essential ingredients for long term success.[25]

In a recent interview, ADM William McRaven, the commander of U.S. Special Operations Command, said, "There is nobody in the U.S. government that thinks we can kill our way to victory . . . What happens is, by capturing and killing some of these high-value targets, we [the military] buy space and time for the rest of the government to work."[26] Both of these senior

---

[24] Robert Gates, "Speech during Landon Lecture" (Speech, Kansas State University, Manhattan, KA, November 26, 2007).

[25] Ibid.

[26] Barton Gellman, "William McRaven: The Admiral," *Time Magazine*, December 26, 2011, 94.

leaders, well steeped in both the country level insurgencies of Iraq and Afghanistan, as well as the global effort to defeat Al Qaeda, have clearly laid out the limitations of military force in counterinsurgencies. During counterinsurgencies, the military creates the time and space for the other instruments of national power to carry out the non-kinetic functions that actually win the wars. In the ongoing global counterinsurgency against Al Qaeda, the rest of the government is not working this problem as efficiently as they could. The Defense Department's contributions could be more effective by identifying the supporting activities ongoing under the defense function, assessing their contributions, and proposing recommendations for future activities.

> Pure military skill is not enough. A full spectrum of military, para-military and civil action must be blended to produce success. The enemy uses economic and political warfare, propaganda and naked military aggression in an endless combination to oppose a free choice of government, and suppress the rights of the individual by terror, by subversion and by force of arms. To win in this struggle, our officers and [service] men must understand and combine the political, economic and civil actions with skilled military efforts in the execution of the mission.[27]

This quote didn't come from the post-9/11 world. It didn't come from those who wrote the new FM 3-24 manual on counterinsurgency. It came from President John F. Kennedy in a letter to the United States Army dated April 11, 1962. This speaks to the timeless nature of these counterinsurgency principles. One of the greatest contributions that the Department of Defense can make is the growth of its warrior-diplomats. A soldier must be equally comfortable in a remote fire base in the mountains of the Hindu Kush as he is dining with the military leadership in a sub-Saharan African country discussing the development of their counterterrorism program and their human rights initiatives. Conversely, diplomats must be equally as comfortable in Paris as they are sitting in a shura with local Afghan village, tribal or religious leaders discussing security, development, religious freedom, and respect for universal rights. Most importantly,

---

[27] President John F. Kennedy, "Speech to the United States Army" (Presidential address, Ft. Bragg, NC, April 11, 1962).

both must be guided by a national strategy that addresses a full spectrum approach to countering the threat that the Al Qaeda Network poses to the country.

What Defense is Doing Now

The defense instrument of national power, carried out or supported by both the Department of Defense and U.S. intelligence agencies, has been effectively disrupting Al Qaeda for well over a decade. Most of these efforts have fallen under counterterrorism operations, building international partner capacity, building and maintaining relationships, and informational activities. These are all critical areas worthy of continued effort although they should be recognized as supporting efforts. Many of these activities fall into the diplomatic or developmental functional areas but, for reasons that will be discussed in those functional sections later in this chapter, the military conducts them out of necessity.

Counterterrorism – Kinetic Operations

Counterterrorism operations, kinetic operations designed to capture or kill high value individuals throughout the Al Qaeda network, are the most well known aspect of the conflict, and have been analyzed and refined to the point that they are enormously successful. As demonstrated during the early morning hours of May 2, 2011, as well as countless other operations in Iraq, Afghanistan, and around the world, the U.S has shown that its military instrument of national power is extraordinarily effective at this kinetic aspect of the current fight. Al Qaeda must understand the determination of the United States to protect its citizens with, if presented with no viable alternative, targeted violence applied in a precise and controlled manner in order to ensure destruction of appropriate targets and to avoid collateral damage. Members of the military and intelligence agencies have conducted these tasks with the utmost professionalism and with great success since 9/11. However, while they realize that their efforts

73

are critical to the eventual defeat of Al Qaeda, they know that theirs is a supporting effort that disrupts ongoing terrorist operations, and creates time and space for the other instruments of national power to actually bring on the demise of Al Qaeda.

Building Partner Capacity

"Arguably the most important component in the War on Terror is not the fighting we do ourselves, but how well we enable and empower our partners to defend and govern themselves. The standing up and mentoring of indigenous army and police – once the province of Special Forces – is now a key mission for the military as a whole."[28] The extensive efforts to build partner capacity, are ongoing throughout the world, and have had significant success in enabling other nations to both address domestic violent extremist concerns and in some cases to deploy their forces outside their borders to assist with regional problems and specifically international issues of mutual interest with the U.S. "Combating violent extremism requires long-term, innovative approaches, and an orchestration of national and international power. By strengthening our partners' security capacity, we will deny terrorists freedom of action and access to resources, while diminishing the conditions that foster violent extremism."[29] As General Ward noted above, these efforts are critical to long term success for several reasons. First, the U.S. does not have the capacity to address the entirety of the Al Qaeda network simultaneously, nor all of the other violent extremist networks, throughout the world. More importantly, as T.E. Lawrence put it in his *27 Articles*, "Better the [locals] do it . . . than you do it . . . It is their war, and you are to help them, not to win it for them. Actually, also, under the very odd conditions of Arabia [and many other locations around the world], your practical work will not be as good as,

---

[28] Gates, Speech during Landon Lecture.

[29] William Ward (General, commander USAFRICOM), "Testimony to the Senate Armed Services Committee on March 17, 2009," http://armed-services.senate.gov/statemnt/2010/03%20March/Ward%2003-09-10.pdf (accessed on Februuary 7, 2012).

perhaps, you think it is."[30] Lawrence's statement accounts for the fact that, while it is a transnational network, Al Qaeda's center of gravity lies within the populations which are best addressed at the local level by other locals. The military has begun to embrace this concept and has been effective in their efforts to build the capacities of host nation forces to enable them to operate independently.

Relationships

The military must continue to foster relationships with mid to senior level leaders throughout the world. General Mattis' relationship with General Tantawi, and Admiral Mullen's relationship with General Kayani in Pakistan are among the very few relationships we have, or had, in those areas. An article written about an impending meeting between General Mattis and General Kayani demonstrates the extent to which these relationships between senior military officers have become so critical to America's foreign relations in the current global environment.

> Officials in the US and Pakistan think that the talks between General Mattis and General Kayani will set off a sequence of negotiations and engagements that will revive the tattered relationships between the two countries.[31]

While this in no way implies that the military should assume responsibility for diplomacy, the military's role in diplomacy must be acknowledged. The military must continue to encourage development and maintenance of strong relationships with foreign military leadership. Language training, cultural awareness, extended tours, and repeat tours to the same geographical areas, are a few of the ways in which the military is addressing this requirement.

Defense Information Efforts

One of the most controversial activities that the military is carrying out are its informational efforts which are best exemplified by Operation OBJECTIVE VOICE.

---

[30] T.E. Lawrence, "Twenty Seven Articles," *Arab Bulletin,* August 20, 1917.
[31] The Express Tribune Web Desk, "U.S. considering formal apology for NATO attacks: Report, General Mattis to meet Kayani," *The Express Tribune*, February 7, 2012.

OBJECTIVE VOICE is "U.S. Africa Command's information operations effort to counter violent extremism by leveraging media capabilities in ways that encourage the public to repudiate extremist ideologies."[32] Its objectives are to:

- Establish effective communications within countries whose populations are susceptible to violent extremist ideology
- Neutralize violent extremist organizations ability to naturalize a system of beliefs
- Increase communication of contradictions with violent extremists' systems of beliefs
- Prevent violent extremist organizations from universalizing the local issues into the narrative
- Degrade the support structure for violent extremist system of beliefs
- Build self-sustaining indigenous partner capability to counter violent extremist ideology[33]

The operation is enabling local leaders to promote a counter narrative that highlights the differences between Al Qaeda's narrative and a more moderate alternative. Africa Command coordinates closely with U.S. embassies, the Department of State, and USAID in the implementation of the program, particularly to ensure that they are capturing the local environments accurately and appropriately. Despite its successes, Operation OBJECTIVE VOICE, and other efforts like it, should be a Department of State endeavor. It is a good example of how the Department of Defense is making contributions in areas not traditionally associated with the military.

Recommendations for Defense

Within its appropriate limitations and with the understanding that it is a supporting effort, the defense functional area of the effort to defeat Al Qaeda has been successful. All ongoing functions should be continued. At the same time, the government must recognize the limitations for the effectiveness of the military against Al Qaeda. Put another way, the government should ask what defense should not be doing. This question has already been answered within the

---

[32] Ward, Testimony March 9, 2010.
[33] Ibid.

military. It is important for the national leadership, and the leadership of other U.S. government departments and agencies, to understand that the military, and even the counterterrorism activities that support them, should not be the main effort in the fight to defeat Al Qaeda.

The wars in Iraq and Afghanistan have served as fuel for Al Qaeda's ideological narrative over the past ten years. The resolution of the two, complete in Iraq and underway in Afghanistan, will do much to quell one of their primary rallying cries. While many of the underlying issues that were the cause for the initial creation of Al Qaeda still exist, focusing military efforts on the areas discussed above, along with resolution of the conflict in Afghanistan will contribute significantly to the eventual defeat of Al Qaeda.

Diplomacy

The Department of State must embrace the idea that this is a global ideological confrontation requiring a diplomatic main effort. It is at the heart of the four objectives critical to defeating Al Qaeda: employing an indirect approach, focusing on the ideology, separating Al Qaeda from the Muslim world, and enhancing the country's capacity to perform those three. They must take the lead in this effort since the main effort falls squarely in their area of responsibility. That diplomatic main effort will require enhanced capacity, more robust engagement with the Muslim world, aggressive diplomacy, better tailored support to counterterrorism operations, and more robust information operations. This section will describe what the Department of State is doing in each of these areas, and make recommendations on how those functions could be improved.

Capacity

The wars in Iraq and Afghanistan have demonstrated the lack of capacity for organizations such as the Department of State and USAID to perform the non-kinetic functions that are required in a counterinsurgency. This has been highlighted by numerous diplomats and military leaders including the Secretaries of State and Defense. Some believe that the requirement will go away once the U.S. completes its withdrawals from Iraq and Afghanistan. On the contrary, there will remain a global requirement to increase our diplomatic and developmental efforts worldwide to fight the global counterinsurgency against Al Qaeda, its associated movements, and the ideology that it stems from. Failure to increase this capacity, as called for by Secretaries Rice, Clinton, Gates, and Panetta, will severely limit the United States' ability to conduct the actions required to ultimately defeat Al Qaeda.

Secretary Gates, during a speech in 2007, expressed concern over the reduction in military and intelligence capabilities following the collapse of the Soviet Union. He went on to say that what was:

> Arguably even more shortsighted, was the gutting of America's ability to engage, assist, and communicate with other parts of the world – the 'soft' power, which had been so important throughout the Cold War. The State Department froze the hiring of new Foreign Service officers for a period of time. The United States Agency for International Development saw deep staff cuts – its permanent staff dropping from a high of 15,000 during Vietnam to about 3,000 in the 1990s.[34]

These reductions following the Cold War impacted the Department's ability to perform its mission overseas. Increased requirements across the board "left U.S. embassy personnel overwhelmed and acutely understaffed."[35] Often the military has stepped in to fill the void created by shortfalls in personnel and resources for diplomacy and development.[36] There is understandably, and appropriately, concern among many that the military is not the correct tool

---

[34] Gates, Speech during Landon Lecture.

[35] Congressional Research Service, *Africa Command: U.S. Strategic Interests and the Role of the U.S. Military in Africa*, 22 July 20011 (Washington, D.C.: Government Printing Office, 2011), 7.

[36] U.S. Department of State and the Broadcasting Board of Governors Office of Inspector, *OIG Report No. ISP-I-09-63, Inspection of the Bureau of African Affairs (August 2009)*, by Office of the Inspector General, Open-file report, Department of State (Washington, D.C., 2009), 8.

for these functions. The Department of State must be better funded in the future in order to grow its capacity to perform this critical role in the effort to defeat Al Qaeda.

Engagement with Muslims

Engagement with Muslims around the world is an important function in the effort to defeat Al Qaeda's ideology, counter their narrative, and isolate them from the their support base within the Muslim world. The Department of State must create better unity within its engagement options, increase its engagement capacity, refocus its engagement efforts beyond the state level, and adjust its overall message. The Department has focused their engagements in this area in the office of the Special Representative to Muslim Communities who has been tasked by the Secretary to engage with Muslims at the community level. At the same time, country teams have the lead on engagement with the governments of Muslim countries. Because many offices have equities in this effort, this engagement should be a unified approach consisting of representation from the Bureau for Counterterrorism, the Special Representative, and regional bureaus and country teams as appropriate. Ultimately, all diplomats should be Special Representatives to the Muslim Community with a common approach directed by a single entity.

The Special Representative to Muslim Communities is only one person who is responsible for engagement with the 1.6B Muslims in the world, 23% of the world's population in 2010 and projected to grow significantly in the future. [37] The Department of State regional bureaus are responsible for much smaller percentages of the world's population and arguably less important segments with respect to the nation's vital interests. The Office of the Special Representative to Muslim Communities should be expanded in size and scope to become the

---

[37] Pew Forum on Religion & Public Life, and Pew Research Center, *The Future of the Global Muslim Population, Projections for 2010-2030,* January 27, 2011, (Washington, D.C.: Pew Research Center, 2011), 1.

Bureau for Muslim Engagement with global responsibility and the authority to engage with any and all Muslim leaders on behalf of the Department.

The most important change that the Department must make in its engagement strategy is its messaging. The Special Representatives efforts to educate the Muslim world about America, and what it does and does not stand for, are quite important, but often leave it up to the listeners to discern how the relationship applies to them. The Department must adopt a more assertive message about how the country desires a peaceful and productive relationship with the Muslim people as long as they are willing to respect the norms of global civilization. However, voicing that narrative through an American speaker, even if it's a Muslim, significantly reduces its effect. As discussed previously, American leaders hold little credibility in a debate over the use of violence in the name of Islam. Muslim leaders throughout the world have written and spoken extensively, but mostly privately or outside of the public eye, about the many ways in which Al Qaeda's ideology is in violation of both the letter and spirit of Islam. The U.S. must encourage mainstream Muslim leaders, who have the credibility within the Muslim world to voice a narrative counter to that of the often popular radical elements and violent extremists, to have this discussion on behalf of the western world. It is both reasonable and critical for the United States to ask those Muslim leaders, and the Muslim population in general, to publically reject and ostracize those radical elements which have enjoyed sanctuary behind them. In the short to mid-term, the country must move more quickly towards a definitive posture, aligned with the voices of mainstream Islam which significantly alters the narrative of the global Muslim population to one that shuns Al Qaeda and its ideology, and other elements of Islam that advocate the use of violence.

Aggressive Diplomacy

How can a man in a cave out communicate the world's leading communications
society?[38]

Richard Holbrooke

The United States must adopt a more aggressive diplomatic approach towards the Muslim
world as described in the Cold War case study. To do this, the Department of State must craft a
clear strategy and policy message, draw a diplomatic "line in the sand", influence Muslims to
isolate Al Qaeda, and influence Muslims to be the voice of their own mainstream narrative. As
the previous section discussed, engaging with and building relationships with Muslims from all
walks of life is important. However, the United States must start asking something of them. The
country must draw "lines in the sand" and ask Muslims to stand with the United States on the
side of freedom, human rights, and representative government. The country must be clear in its
expectation of legitimate, representational governments that respect the rights of their citizens
and provide for their needs. This speaks to their long standing grievances against repressive, but
stabilizing, regimes with which the United States has allied itself in the past. It will encourage
acceptance within Muslim communities for the United States' message. Addressing this
grievance, by advocating the freedoms mentioned above, without dictating an expectation of an
American style democracy, will result in a Muslim population that will be more welcoming of a
productive relationship with the United States and more likely to champion a mainstream
narrative that isolates Al Qaeda and its associated movements.

Islamic extremists have been so successful in their public relations campaign that they
have successfully manipulated the Western press into perpetuating their victimhood status,

---

[38] National Commission on Terrorist Attacks upon the United States, 377.

contributing to the sense of disrespect that is fueling Muslim extremism.[39] The United States

must stop ignoring this out of a misplaced sense of guilt, and aggressively counter it. The 9/11

Commission recognized this and was clear about it in its report:

> Just as we did in the Cold War, we need to defend our ideals abroad vigorously. America does need to stand up for its values [and should not feel ashamed for it] . . . If the United States does not act aggressively to define itself in the Islamic world, the extremists will gladly do the job for us.[40]

An example of a missed opportunity for this kind of diplomacy occurred in June 2004 when a

representative of the Saudi Arabian government openly called for a government sponsored jihad

against Al Qaeda and its associated movements within Saudi Arabia.[41] The report cited

numerous shootouts between those elements and the Saudi security forces. This was a perfect

opportunity for the Department of State's senior leadership to engage with and publicize this

theme, not just within the United States and Saudi Arabia but worldwide. The counter argument

to this kind of aggressive diplomatic activity is that it plays into Al Qaeda's narrative about ties

between the American government and the "apostate" Saudi government. While this may be

true at face value, and it may be received well within extremist circles, it is critical for the

mainstream Muslim population worldwide to hear that side of the story.

Support to Military Counterterrorism Efforts

The Department of State has been actively involved in counterterrorism efforts against Al

Qaeda and its associate movements since 9/11. Their contributions have been critical to the

enormously successful worldwide operations which have significantly disrupted the networks

and prevented them from conducting any major attacks since then. The Department should

---

[39] Dawn Perlmutter, "Mujahideen Desecration: Beheadings, Mutilation & Muslim Iconoclasm," *Anthropoetics* 12, no. 2 (Fall 2006 / Winter 2007), http://www.anthropoetics.ucla.edu/ap1202/muja07.htm (accessed February 24, 2012).

[40] National Commission on Terrorist Attacks upon the United States, 377.

[41] Ibid., 373.

continue these efforts, while recognizing that it is a supporting effort to the overall effort to defeat Al Qaeda. Too often, the Department of State's focus for addressing Al Qaeda, and other violent extremist organizations, appears to be support for military counterterrorism operations. On their website, the Department's Bureau of Counterterrorism lists the ten things they want Americans to know about the bureau.[42] Most of the items relate to direct approaches, either supporting United States led counterterrorism efforts, or engaging with partner nations to support their counterterrorism efforts. While both of these are productive, the second is more so than the first, and they are both secondary efforts to the larger global effort to counter Al Qaeda's ideology. Nowhere does it mention countering the ideology. The Bureau for Counterterrorism should be leading the way for the Department in their effort to defeat Al Qaeda. With the consolidation of the Department's global violent extremism expertise in one bureau, they should be able to analyze the ideology, dissect the narrative, develop a strategy to defeat Al Qaeda's ideology from the diplomacy perspective, and work with country teams to implement the strategy.

The Department of State has been involved in several recent or ongoing diplomatic efforts to counter Al Qaeda. One of these is an event co-sponsored by the U.S. and Turkey, the Global Counterterrorism Forum. This forum wrote the *Cairo Declaration on Counterterrorism and the Rule of Law: Effective Counterterrorism Practice in the Criminal Justice Sector*, thus creating an impressive achievement in improving global cooperation and furthering a counter ideology.[43] Unfortunately, like so many previous documents, it focuses on actions required of governments and their dealings with their populations and domestic extremist organizations.

---

[42] U.S. Department of State, "Bureau of Counterterrorism website," U.S. Department of State, http://www.state.gov/j/ct/index.htm (accessed on February 15, 2012).

[43] Global Counterterrorism Forum, "Cairo Declaration on Counterterrorism and the Rule of Law: Effective Counterterrorism Practice in the Criminal Justice Sector, September 22, 2012," U.S. Department of State, http://www.state.gov/documents/organization/173159.pdf (accessed February 15, 2012).

The expectations for governments emphasizing justice, liberty, and rule of law for their citizens are important, because it has been recognized that repressive regimes, which do not respect the rights of their citizens create the conditions for violent extremist ideology to thrive. However, the Declaration does not focus on the Muslim population, which is the most important element in this global counterinsurgency. Clear expectations for Muslims to isolate Al Qaeda and denounce their extremist ideology should be added to the Declaration as well as any other guidance documents like it with which the Department is associated.

Another, better known counterterrorism support function that the Department is leading is the Trans-Sahara Counterterrorism Partnership. The partnership is a program aimed at defeating Al Qaeda, and other violent extremist organizations, in the Pan-Sahel and Maghreb countries. Its objectives are to build the capacity of partner nations to conduct counterterrorism operations; enhance and institutionalize cooperation amongst the region's security forces; promote democratic governance; discredit violent extremist ideology; and to reinforce bilateral military ties with the United States.[44] It does give mention to the important task of discrediting the ideology, but the main effort of the program is the military function of building partner nation capacity to conduct counterterrorism operations. While not necessarily targeting the root of the problem, the Partnership has been quite successful in enabling the countries of the region to take a more proactive role in addressing internal security challenges that they face from domestic or transnational violent extremist organizations. These counterterrorism support functions are important to the military's effort to disrupt Al Qaeda and its associated movements in order to provide time and space for the other functions to defeat them.

---

[44] Congressional Research Service, 23.

Informational Activities

Ideology, ideology, ideology: the Department of State must take the lead in U.S.

government efforts to defeat Al Qaeda's ideology through informational activities. To do this,

they must: regain and own the narrative, recognize that words matter, and reestablish the U.S.

Information Agency to grow and professionalize the country's information experts. The U.S.

does not currently "own" the narrative, which is critical to defeating Al Qaeda's ideology. Al

Qaeda, and its associated movements, remain several steps ahead of the United States when it

comes to information operations and spreading the narrative of their ideology. The United States

must regain the initiative in the informational realm because without it, Al Qaeda will be free to

spread their ideology which will in turn continue to expand their influence and virtually

guarantee their continued existence. The percentages of favorable opinions of the United States,

within Muslim countries, is less than impressive. In a 2003 survey, over 60% of Turks polled

were very or somewhat fearful that the United States might attack them.[45] Obviously the U.S.

had no intention of doing so, but lost the narrative and was unable to communicate effectively

with the Turkish population. There are already credible opportunities to conduct this sort of

effective communication with Muslim audiences, primarily by being proactive in helping

mainstream Muslims get their message out. One of these opportunities is the New Mardin

Declaration, written by attendees of the Mardin Conference in 2010, which has gone relatively

unnoticed. [46] The Mardin Conference was a watershed event that brought together Muslim

scholars and religious leaders to discuss the Mardin *fatwa*, written by Ibn Tamiyyah in the early

---

[45] National Commission on Terrorist Attacks upon the United States, 375. A more recent Pew opinion poll showed that only 10% of Turks had a favorable opinion of the U.S. as of 2011 (online at Pew Research Center, *Pew Global Attitudes Project*, accessed on June 9, 2012 from http://www.pewglobal.org/database/?indicator=1&country=224).

[46] Mardin Conference, "Background information on conference," Mardin Conference, http://www.mardin-fatwa.com/about.php (accessed January 17, 2012).

1300s, which is a critical document for Al Qaeda's narrative and ideology. The conference

members examined several aspects of Ibn Tamiyyah's *fatwa*, but the primary concern was to

understand it in the context of the time it was written in order to translate that context, and

therefore his original intent, into the modern age. Their conclusions, controversial among some

Muslims who lean towards supporting extremist organizations, were that:

> Ibn Tamiyyah's *fatwa* concerning Mardin can under no circumstances be
> appropriated and used as evidence for leveling the charge of *kufr* [unbelief]
> against fellow Muslims, rebelling against rulers, deeming game their lives and
> property, terrorizing those who enjoy safety and security, acting treacherously
> towards those who live (in harmony) with fellow Muslims or with whom fellow
> Muslims live (in harmony) via the bond of citizenship and peace.[47]

The New Mardin Declaration, while not perfect, was an impressive effort on the part of

mainstream Muslims to regain the narrative from Al Qaeda. More important than its many other

merits, it carries legitimacy in the Muslim world. It was not written through an American voice,

an international voice from the western world, or even a Muslim voice from either of those. The

signatories to the New Mardin Declaration carried legitimate religious and scholarly credentials

recognized and respected in the Muslim world. This effort, by mainstream Muslims to define

what they want their religion to be in the modern world, is an example of the informational

opportunities that the United States must capitalize on in the future in order to regain the

narrative.

To increase the country's ability to regain the narrative and ultimately defeat Al Qaeda's

ideology, the U.S. must regrow its informational mechanisms. The Cold War case study showed

that organizations such as the U.S. Information Agency were critical in countering and ultimately

defeating the communist ideology. The current formal U.S. information efforts are dominated by

organizations other than the Department of State, as shown by Operation OBJECTIVE VOICE

---

[47] Mardin Conference, "New Mardin Declaration, 2006," Mardin Conference, http://www.mardin-fatwa.com/about.php (accessed January 17, 2012), 2.

in Africa. The Department of State has consolidated responsibility for its informational activities in the Bureau for International Information Programs which interacts with and supports the country teams, but has no directive authority over them in order to drive a unified message. Without a separate entity with responsibility for the informational function, it is often subordinated to other priorities and is disjointed in execution because there is no mechanism to direct a cohesive message. In the near term, the Department of State must become more directive towards its embassies when it comes to regional approaches to transnational issues. The country teams would still be required to take the initiative to implement those programs in accordance with the unique characteristics of their assigned countries, but a regional approach would provide a far more beneficial long term effect. In the longer term, the country must address the fact that there is no effective, and empowered, coordinator of U.S. information programs overseas. A separate agency responsible, and empowered with the appropriate authorities, for planning, coordinating and implementing this effort would lead a far more effective counter to Al Qaeda's informational and propaganda activities.

Recommendations for Diplomacy

These recommendations will improve the United States' approach to defeating Al Qaeda. The United States must recognize that the main effort is a diplomatic one, and appropriately focus and resource its diplomacy, thus enabling the country to make significant progress towards defeating the network. This will require enhancing the capacity of the Department of State to carry out these critical functions overseas, both by growing the Foreign Service corps and by growing its overall budget. This enlarged Foreign Service corps must refocus its engagement to expand relationships with religious and tribal leaders who have significant influence in many Muslim countries. The United States must develop a more aggressive diplomatic stance that supports a new National Strategy for Combating Terrorism by communicating clear expectations for the international community, Muslims worldwide, and Al Qaeda. The Department must redesignate its own main effort away from counterterrorism while maintaining critical support to those operations. Finally, the Department should bring back the U.S. Information Agency in order to provide a single point of direction for a coordinated information effort throughout the government. These changes will enable the Department of State to focus their efforts on an indirect approach to defeat Al Qaeda by more effectively countering their ideology and isolating them from the Muslim world. Department of State leadership of these critical functions will ensure recognition of these as the main effort.

Currently efforts to defeat Al Qaeda, even at DoS, are focused on kinetic targeting, building relationships to further enable U.S. kinetic targeting or to enable other countries with intelligence to target unilaterally, and building capacity so that developing countries can conduct operations on their own in the future. Everyone seems to be ignoring the Muslim population itself. Al Qaeda's ideology cannot be defeated by kinetic action. Kinetic action and enabling activities, on the part of the United States and its allies, disrupt future terrorist attacks but they don't address the ideology that fuels the attacks. Until the ideology is addressed, cells all over the world will continue to grow their ranks, plan attacks, and execute attacks whenever and wherever possible. It is in this ideological arena that Al Qaeda will be truly defeated but, as yet, the western world has only tentatively entered that arena, and only for occasional short forays. The national strategy to defeat Al Qaeda and its associated movements, and in fact all militant Islamist groups sharing that ideology, must shift its main effort to a robust ideological confrontation with a supporting kinetic effort.

Development

The development function is more limited than defense or diplomacy, but nonetheless

serves a critical role in the effort to defeat Al Qaeda. The most important issue for the

development function is the question, "Development to what end?" The Cold War case study

described the reasons that President Kennedy created the U.S. Agency for International

Development in 1961. He advocated first the values based justification that in itself supports one

of the four national interests listed in the 2010 National Security Strategy.[48] He described as

more important the second justification, which was one of a realist approach to foreign policy

noting that aid and development targeted at countries and regions susceptible to violent

extremism (totalitarianism in President Kennedy's case) were productive in preventing the

spread of those ideologies and thus cost effective in the long run.

The United States relearned the importance of the development function, and a competent

organization to oversee and execute it, in the years following 9/11. Interestingly, much of this

recognition has come from military leadership. Secretary Gates noted that "one of the most

important lessons from our experience in Iraq, Afghanistan, and elsewhere has been the decisive

role reconstruction, development, and governance play in any meaningful, long-term success."[49]

The military, both in Iraq and Afghanistan, as well as other regions of the world in which Al

Qaeda has extended their influence, has recognized that the defense function is unable to achieve

victory in this conflict unassisted. General Petraeus acknowledged this with his 80/20

formulation: "To succeed in counterinsurgency, 80% of funding and focus should be on political

---

[48] U.S. President, *National Security Strategy 2010* (Washington, D.C.: Government Printing Office, May 2010), 7.

[49] Gates, Speech during Landon Lecture.

activities and only 20% on providing security." [50] He went on to lament the fact that the

Department of Defense, until the recent budget crisis, has been relatively well funded for their

part in this conflict but that, despite calls from both Department of Defense and State leadership,

Congress had not funded the Department of State or USAID as advised. An analysis of the

USAID operating budgets following 9/11, shows that they did not grow measurably until

FY2010, in spite of what would appear to have been an exponential growth in requirements for

their services in support of U.S. foreign policy.[51] The Cold War showed that "vigorous

diplomacy, made possible by foreign aid, is the cheapest and most enduring means to exercise

geopolitical leadership," and to positively influence susceptible populations in support of U.S.

foreign policy.[52] Unfortunately, it is difficult to prove to budget conscious congressional

leadership that development programs have contributed to successes, or even harder to prove that

they have prevented susceptible populations from succumbing to extremist ideology. Military

statistics such as numbers of high value individuals captured or killed are easy to demonstrate,

but merely represent outputs. Increased numbers of Muslims convinced to isolate Al Qaeda and

its associated movements are positive outcomes, but ones that are quite difficult to demonstrate

tangibly.

    In the future, development priorities should include expanding the role of development in

U.S. foreign policy, and increasing USAID's capacity to do so. In their new role, they should

become more aggressive in linking their actions to foreign policy. The values based

development that President Kennedy talked about is important in communicating American

---

[50] Micah Zenko and Rebecca R. Friedman, "A soft power bargain: A fully funded foreign aid budget is essential to prevent the political instability and violent conflict that harms American security," Los Angeles Times, February 16, 2011.

[51] U.S. Department of State, "Summary and Highlights of International Affairs (Function 150) Budget Request (Budget requests from FY2001-FY2012)," U.S. Department of State, http://www.state.gov/s/d/rm/rls/iab/index.htm (accessed on February 15, 2012).

[52] Zenko and Friedman.

values to the world, but more important is an aggressive development program that directly supports the country's current priority of separating Al Qaeda from the global Muslim population. They are already doing much of this as seen in their programs to empower communications networks, targeting infrastructure improvement programs, and teaching countries how to develop independent economies. In the budget constrained future, these programs must be carefully examined to ensure that they are effectively focused to contribute directly to U.S. foreign policy goals, rather than to supporting a generic values based program. Finally, their capacity must be increased significantly, both in budget and in manpower. USAID in the future should mirror the organization that the United States built during the Cold War so that it can make similarly significant contributions to U.S. foreign policy and the effort to defeat Al Qaeda and their ideology.

This page intentionally left blank

CONCLUSION

Al Qaeda and its associated movements represent a long-term threat to the United States and its allies around the world. The U.S. must adopt a new approach towards Al Qaeda centered around a global counterinsurgency that focuses on employing an indirect approach, defeating Al Qaeda's ideology, isolating them from the worldwide Muslim population, and greatly expanding the country's capacity to perform those functions. Al Qaeda is incorrectly identified as a "terrorist" organization, a characterization that perpetuates the current approach. They employ violence, terrorism, as a tool to achieve their political goals, meeting the classic definition of an insurgency but on a global scale. Historical counterinsurgencies have shown that direct confrontations are rarely successful. They require indirect approaches that are founded in a clear policy, focused on the population, and sufficiently resourced. As a global insurgency, Al Qaeda must be defeated through a global counterinsurgency rather than the traditional counterterrorism methods which been the primary approach up to this point.

The three case studies examined, the Cold War, the Cuban Missile Crisis, and CJTF-HOA, demonstrated several historical parallels, which were used to identify lessons that can be applied to the current conflict with Al Qaeda. The Cold War demonstrated the importance of building organizations to defeat ideologies, and that the main effort must be the ideology with all other efforts supporting it. It also showed that ideological confrontations take time and that short-term commitments will not be productive to the overall effort. On the negative side, the Cold War identified the over reliance on the military which has grown in U.S. foreign policy and continues to plague the country throughout the conflict with Al Qaeda. The Cuban Missile Crisis showed the effectiveness of aggressive diplomacy in dealing with ideologically driven opponents. It also showed the need for a clear understanding of the enemy's motivations to

93

develop an appreciation for their perspective. Finally, it showed that it is critical to have an understanding of the enemy's perception of the U.S., as well as the non-aligned population's perception of the U.S. CJTF-HOA has shown that a long-term commitment, with relatively limited resources, employing a regionally focused indirect approach, that interweaves the functions of defense, diplomacy, and development, can have a significant positive impact. All of these are important lessons in developing and implementing a more effective approach to defeat Al Qaeda and its associated movements.

The new approach must be guided by a national strategy that focuses all of the elements of national power on the indirect approach to defeat Al Qaeda's ideology and to separate them from the Muslim world. It must also incorporate the lessons learned from the case studies. The defense functions have been successful in the tasks asked of it, but the limitation of its utility in this global counterinsurgency are important to understand. The diplomatic and development functions are critical to the defeat of Al Qaeda and they must be expanded significantly to provide the capacity required for the new approach. Engagement activities with the Muslim world must be expanded, informational activities should be brought under the control of an organization dedicated to that function, and U.S. diplomacy must assume an aggressive approach. Finally, development functions under USAID have been extremely successful, but their effectiveness has been limited by their lack of capacity.

Al Qaeda and its associated movements can be defeated. The new approach towards Al Qaeda must focus on indirect methods, Al Qaeda's ideology, and isolating them from the rest of the Muslim population. These efforts will necessitate increasing the capacity of those departments and agencies within the U.S. government, other than the military, that perform those functions.

BIBLIOGRAPHY

Abizaid, John. "Slide briefed to the Senate Armed Services Committee by General Abizaid on September 29, 2005." http://www.flickr.com/photos/mideaststrategy (accessed February 7, 2012).

Amend, Kurt. "Counterinsurgency Principles for the Diplomat." *Small Wars Journal* (July 2008).

Bacevich, Andrew. "Speech to Massachusetts Institute of Technology - Center for International Studies." Speech, Massachusetts Institute of Technology, Boston, MA, September 14, 2010.

Baltazar, Thomas and Elisabeth Kvitashvili. "Combating Terrorism: The Role of USAID and Development Assistance." *Marine Corps Gazette*, Web Article (April 2007).

Bergen, Peter. *Holy War, Inc.: Inside the Secret World of Osama Bin Laden.* New York: Free Press, 2001.

---. *The Longest War: The Enduring Conflict Between America and Al-Qaeda.* New York: Free Press, 2011.

---. *The Osama Bin Laden I Know: An Oral History of Al-Qaeda's Leader.* New York: Free Press, 2006.

Bin Laden, Usama. "Declaration of Jihad Against the United States." Al-Islah (Internet), September 2, 1996. As analyzed in Michael Scheuer. *Osama bin Laden.* New York: Oxford University Press, 2011.

---. "Jihad Against Jews and Crusaders." Originally published by the al Quds al Arabi newspaper on February 23, 1998. PBS Online, http://www.pbs.org/newshour/terrorism/international/fatwa_1998.html (accessed on February 21, 2012).

Birtle, Andrew. *U.S. Army Counterinsurgency and Contingency Operations Doctrine 1942– 1976.* Washington, D.C.: Government Printing Office, 2006.

British Broadcasting Company. "Somalia's al-Shabab Join al-Qaeda." BBC News Online, http://www.bbc.co.uk/news/world-africa-16979440 (accessed on February 10, 2012).

Bush, George. "Speech at the National Cathedral." Presidential address, Washington, D.C., September 14, 2001.

---. "Speech to a joint session of Congress." Presidential address, Washington, D.C., September 20, 2001.

---. "Speech at the U.S. Military Academy." Presidential address, West Point, NY, June 1, 2002.

---. "Speech at the National Endowment for Democracy." Presidential address, Washington, D.C., October 6, 2005.

Carpenter, Scott. *Fighting the Ideological Battle: The Missing Link in U.S. Strategy to Counter Violent Extremism.* Washington, D.C.: Washington Institute for Near East Policy, 2010.

Combined Joint Task Force – Horn of Africa. "CJTF-HOA Fact Sheet." CJTF-HOA. http://www.hoa.africom.mil/pdfFiles/Fact%20Sheet.pdf (accessed February 15, 2012).

Congressional Research Service. *Africa Command: U.S. Strategic Interests and the Role of the U.S. Military in Africa, 22 July 2011.* Washington, D.C.: Government Printing Office, 2011.

Eikmeier, Dale. "Qutbism: An Ideology of Islamic-Fascism." *Parameters*, Spring 2007.

Galula, David. *Counterinsurgency Warfare: Theory and Practice.* New York: Praeger, 1964.

Gates, Robert. "A Balanced Strategy: Reprogramming the Pentagon for a New Age." *Foreign Affairs*, January/February 2009.

---. "Speech during Landon Lecture." Speech, Kansas State University, Manhattan, KA, November 26, 2007.

Gellman, Barton. "William McRaven: The Admiral." *Time Magazine* (December 26, 2011): 94-100.

Global Counterterrorism Forum. "Cairo Declaration on Counterterrorism and the Rule of Law: Effective Counterterrorism Practice in the Criminal Justice Sector, September 22, 2012." U.S. Department of State. http://www.state.gov/documents/organization/173159.pdf (accessed February 15, 2012).

Ham, Carter. "Testimony to the Senate Armed Services Committee on April 5, 2011." U.S. Congress, 2011.

Jenkins, Brian, and John Godges. *The Long Shadow of 9/11: America's Response to Terrorism.* Santa Monica, CA: RAND, 2011.

Kennedy, John F. "Radio and Television Report to the American People on the Soviet Arms Buildup in Cuba." Presidential address, Washington, D.C., October 22, 1962.

---. "Special Message to Congress on Foreign Aid." Presidential address, Washington, D.C., March 22, 1961.

---. "Speech to U.S. Army personnel." Presidential address, Ft. Bragg, NC, April 11, 1962.

Kepel, Gilles, and Jean-Pierre Milelli, ed. *Al Qaeda in Its Own Words*. Cambridge, Mass: Belknap Press of Harvard University Press, 2009.

Kilcullen, David. "Countering Global Insurgency." *Journal of Strategic Studies*, 28.4 (2005): 597-617.

Killebrew, Robert, ed. "The Country Team in American Strategy." Washington, D.C.: Department of State/Department of Defense, December, 2006.

Kull, Steven. *Feeling Betrayed: The Roots of Muslim Anger at America*. Washington, D.C: Brookings Institution Press, 2011.

Lawrence, T.E. "Twenty Seven Articles." *Arab Bulletin.* August 20, 1917.

Lewis, Bernard. *The Crisis of Islam: Holy War and Unholy Terror*. New York: Random House Trade Paperbacks, 2004.

Long, Austin. *On "Other War": Lessons from Five Decades of Rand Counterinsurgency Research*. Santa Monica, CA: RAND, 2006.

Losey, Brian. "Conflict Prevention in East Africa: The Indirect Approach." *Prism*, Vol 2, No. 2 (March 2011): 77-90.

Mardin Conference. "Background information on conference." Mardin Conference. http://www.mardin-fatwa.com/about.php (accessed January 17, 2012).

---. "New Mardin Declaration, 2006." Mardin Conference. http://www.mardin-fatwa.com/about.php (accessed January 17, 2012).

Marine Corps University. *Al-Qaida After Ten Years of War: A Global Perspective of Successes, Failures and Prospects*. Quantico, VA: Marine Corps University, 2011.

Melshen, Paul. "Mapping Out a Counterinsurgency Campaign Plan: Critical Considerations in Counterinsurgency Campaigning." *Small Wars & Insurgencies*, 18:4, (2007): 668-673.

Nance, Malcolm. *An End to Al Qaeda: Destroying Bin Laden's Jihad and Restoring America's Honor*. New York: St. Martin's Press, 2010.

Naji, Abu Bakr. "Management of Savagery: The Most Critical Stage Through Which the Umma will Pass." Tanslated by William McCants. http://www.wcfia.harvard.edu/olin/images/Management%20of%20Savagery%20-%2005-23-2006.pdf (accessed February 21, 2012).

National Commission on Terrorist Attacks upon the United States. *The 9/11 Commission Report: Final Report of the National Commission on Terrorist Attacks Upon the United States.* New York: Norton, 2004.

Natsios, Andrew. "Testimony to the Senate Foreign Relations Committee on April 1, 2009." U.S. Congress 2009.

Obama, Barak. "Speech to the Turkish National Assembly." Presidential address, Turkish National Assembly Complex, Ankara, Turkey, April 6, 2009.

Olson, Eric. "A Balanced Approach to Irregular Warfare." *The Journal of International Security Affairs*, no. 16, Spring 2009.

Oracle Think Quest Education Foundation. "Cuban Missile Crisis Timeline." Oracle Think Quest Education Foundation. http://library.thinkquest.org/11046/days/timeline.html (accessed on February 15, 2012).

Organization for Security and Cooperation in Europe. "Secretariat – Action Against Terrorism Unit." OSCE. http://www.osce.org/atu/45995 (accessed January 29, 2012).

Paget, Julian. *Counter-insurgency Operations: Techniques of Guerrilla Warfare.* New York: Walker, 1967.

Pew Forum on Religion & Public Life, and Pew Research Center. *The Future of the Global Muslim Population, Projections for 2010-2030,* January 27, 2011. Washington, D.C.: Pew Research Center, 2011.

Perlmutter, Dawn. "Mujahideen Desecration: Beheadings, Mutilation & Muslim Iconoclasm." *Anthropoetics* 12, no. 2 (Fall 2006 / Winter 2007).

Powell, Colin. "Speech to U.N. Security Council." (Speech, New York, NY, November 12, 2001).

Qutb, Sayyid. "Milestones." http://majalla.org/books/2005/qutb-milestone.pdf (accessed on February 21, 2012).

Rabasa, Angel. "Where are we in the 'War of Ideas'?." In *The Long Shadow of 9/11*. Edited by Brian Jenkins and John Godges. Santa Monica: RAND Corporation, 2011.

Reagan, Ronald. "Speech at the Brandenburg Gate." Presidential address, Berlin, GE, June 12, 1987.

Scheuer, Michael. *Imperial Hubris: Why the West is Losing the War on Terror.* Washington, D.C.: Potomac Books Inc, 2004.

---. *Osama bin Laden.* New York: Oxford University Press, 2011.

---. *Through Our Enemies' Eyes: Osama Bin Laden, Radical Islam, and the Future of America.* Washington, D.C.: Potomac Books, Inc, 2006.

Szrom, Charlie, and Chris Harnisch. *Al Qaeda's Operating Environments: A New Approach to the War on Terror.* Washington, DC: American Enterprise Institute, 2011.

The Express Tribune Web Desk. "US considering formal apology for NATO attacks: Report, Gen Mattis to meet Kayani." *The Express Tribune.* February 7, 2012.

U.S. Congress. House. Committee on Armed Services. *Implications of the National Intelligence Estimate regarding al Qaeda.* 110th Cong., 1st sess., July 25, 2007.

---. *The threat posed by al Qaida in the Arabian Peninsula and other regions.* 110th Cong., 2nd sess., January 20, 2010.

---. *Al Qaida in 2010: How should the U.S. respond?.* 110th Cong., 2nd sess., January 27, 2010.

U.S. Department of Defense. *2006 Quadrennial Defense Review.* Washington, D.C.: Department of Defense, 2006.

---. *2010 Quadrennial Defense Review.* Washington, D.C.: Department of Defense, 2010.

U.S. Department of Homeland Security. *Terminology to Define the Terrorists: Recommendations from American Muslims.* Washington, D.C.: Department of Homeland Security, January 2008.

U.S. Department of State. "Bureau of Counterterrorism website." U.S. Department of State. http://www.state.gov/j/ct/index.htm (accessed on February 15, 2012).

---. *Strategic Plan (Fiscal years 2007-2012): Transformational Diplomacy.* Washington, D.C.: Department of State, 2007.

---. "Summary and Highlights of International Affairs (Function 150) Budget Request (Budget requests from FY2001-FY2012)." U.S. Department of State. http://www.state.gov/s/d/rm/rls/iab/index.htm (accessed on February 15, 2012).

U.S. Department of State and the Broadcasting Board of Governors Office of Inspector. *OIG Report No. ISP-I-09-63, Inspection of the Bureau of African Affairs (August 2009)*, by Office of the Inspector General, Open-file report, Department of State (Washington, D.C., 2009).

U.S. Department of the Army. *Counterinsurgency Operations,* Field Manual 3-24. Washington, D.C.: Department of the Army, 2006.

U.S. Information Agency. "USIA Fact Sheet." USIA.
      http://dosfan.lib.uic.edu/usia/usiahome/factshe.htm (accessed February 15, 2012).

U.S. Joint Chiefs of Staff. *Counterinsurgency Operations,* Joint Publication 3-24. Washington,
      D.C.: Joint Chiefs of Staff, 2009.

U.S. President. *National Security Strategy 2002.* Washington, D.C.: Government Printing
      Office, September 2002.

---. *National Security Strategy 2010.* Washington, D.C.: Government Printing Office, May 2010.

---. *National Strategy for Combating Terrorism – 2003.* Washington, D.C.: Government Printing
      Office, 2003.

---. *National Strategy for Combating Terrorism – 2006.* Washington, D.C.: Government Printing
      Office, 2006.

---. *National Strategy for Combating Terrorism – 2011.* Washington, D.C.: Government Printing
      Office, 2011.

Ward, Blake. "Osama's Wake: The Second Generation of Al Qaeda." *Counterproliferation
      Papers,* Future Warfare Series, no. 32 (August 2005).

Ward, William. "Testimony to the Senate Armed Services Committee on March 17, 2009." U.S.
      Congress, 2009.

---. "Testimony to the Senate Armed Services Committee on March 9, 2010." U.S. Congress,
      2010.

Wiersma, Kurt and Ben Larson. "Fourteen Days in October: The Cuban Missile Crisis."
      http://library.thinkquest.org/11046/media/fourteen_days_in_october.pdf (accessed
      February 15, 2012).

Wright, Lawrence. *The Looming Tower: Al-Qaeda and the Road to 9/11.* New York: Knopf,
      2006.

Zawahiri, Ayman al- to Abu Musab al-Zarqawi. Letter written on July 9, 2005.
      http://patriotpost.us/reference/zawahiri-letter (accessed February 21, 2012).

Zenko, Micah and Rebecca R. Friedman. "A soft power bargain: A fully funded foreign aid
      budget is essential to prevent the political instability and violent conflict that harms
      American security." *Los Angeles Times* (February 16, 2011).

www.ingramcontent.com/pod-product-compliance
Lightning Source LLC
Chambersburg PA
CBHW081839280526
45789CB00007B/2501